St. Norbert College Library

DePere, WI

PELIC

D0803060

321.644
C221

GIAMPIERO CAROCCI

ITALIAN FASCISM

Translated by
Isabel Quigly

Penguin Books

Penguin Books Ltd, Harmondsworth, Middlesex, England
Penguin Books Inc., 7110 Ambassador Road, Baltimore, Maryland 21207, U.S.A.
Penguin Books Australia Ltd, Ringwood, Victoria, Australia
Penguin Books Canada Ltd, 41 Steelcase Road West, Markham, Ontario, Canada
Penguin Books (N.Z.) Ltd, 182–190 Wairau Road, Auckland 10, New Zealand

—

Storia del fascismo first published by Editore Aldo Garzanti 1972
This translation published in Pelican Books 1975

—

Copyright © Editore Aldo Garzanti, 1972
Translation copyright © Penguin Books Ltd, 1974

—

Made and printed in Great Britain by
C. Nicholls & Company Ltd
Set in Linotype Juliana

This book is sold subject to the condition
that it shall not, by way of trade or otherwise,
be lent, re-sold, hired out, or otherwise circulated
without the publisher's prior consent in any form of
binding or cover other than that in which it is
published and without a similar condition
including this condition being imposed
on the subsequent purchaser

CONTENTS

I

ORIGINS

THE 1914–1918 war, the Great War, had flung the old Europe into a profoundly critical condition. Never before had its economy and society and the nation states of which it was composed undergone any trials so intense. Never before had such vast numbers of men felt aware, in the trenches, that they themselves were having a direct effect upon political life. The nineteenth century was over, and so – retreating further and further into the distance – was the age known nostalgically as *la belle époque*. Hard times loomed ahead for both liberal institutions and the capitalist economy, which had reached a degree of concentration also never known before. Everywhere – in varying degrees and ways, but everywhere – great innovations were taking place in economic structures, in class relationships, in political institutions, in social behaviour.

A tremendous revolution had taken place in Russia, helped on by the particular weakness of the Russian middle classes and by other historical and political factors. In considering other nations, a distinction has to be drawn between conquerors and conquered. In the vanquished countries, upheavals in general, and the revolutionary pressures of the socialist and communist movements, were far more violent than they were among the victors. But everywhere these movements proved incapable of achieving, or consolidating, power. In the victorious countries, especially France and Britain, the ruling classes, after waging the war in the name of democratic ideals, were concerned most of all to weaken Germany, to shore up their tottering colonies, and to assure themselves of new sources of raw materials and new markets. With these power politics, the background of which was clearly conservative, they sought to overcome post–war difficulties in social and economic affairs. They were only partly successful.

These difficulties were at their worst in Italy, of all the victorious countries. To Italy as to the other victors, the peace treaties had brought some advantages (the full attainment of national aspirations, for instance) and some disadvantages (with regard to the colonies and mandates, and in the supply of raw materials). The advantages, indeed, outweighed the disadvantages; these disadvantages really lay only in the fact that the provision of raw materials had not been made any easier. Indeed, the administration of new colonies or mandates was to become a drain on the Italian economy, rather than an advantage. On the other hand, the disappearance of the Austro-Hungarian empire not only gave Italy a national security unknown to the other victorious powers, but for the first time in its history made Italy a truly great power, with the prospect of playing a leading role and expanding peacefully towards the Danube and the Balkans. This role and this prospect were clearly understood by Count Sforza, Foreign Minister in 1920–21. But they were misinterpreted and the chances of achieving them were lost by Mussolini's diplomacy, and France replaced Italy as the leading power in that area. Political and social troubles began in Italy in the early months of 1919, when the whole country was pervaded by a discontent and an uneasiness similar to those found in the defeated countries. The reasons for this were complex.

Italy had entered the war against the wishes of the majority in parliament and in the country, although its entry was supported by some of the middle and lower-middle classes and, later, by the industrialists. This entry was achieved, with the king's consent, through a show of strength by the conservative Salandra, vociferously supported by a mixed minority made up of idealists, democrats, nationalists, trade unionists and some ex-socialists under the leadership of Mussolini.

Two motives inspired the conduct of the war in Italy: the first was the democratic ideas of the irredentist territories (the Trentino and Istria), and the wish to make freedom and justice triumphant throughout the world; the second was a wish for the expansion of power. During the war, the first motive was the more important; in the post-war period, the second prevailed. The great majority of the bourgeoisie, especially the middle and lower-middle sectors, had supported the war and its objectives, often enthusiastically, whereas the workers and peasants had felt mainly its burdens and the suffering it brought them. When it was over, the country was divided into two: on the one hand, those who had wished for or had supported the war, on the other, those who had not.

The war had been an experience which affected everyone in all the countries which had fought in it; but in Italy, where there was little modern tradition in civil and political life, this experience was particularly profound. There, the war had been the first movement which had really united public opinion; but it had united it by showing up the opposition of *interventisti and disfattisti*, those in favour of and those against the war. This opposition might have been reconciled by the state's authority. But although the state had emerged from the war with increased power, particularly in economic matters, it was also separated from the country in general more than ever before, impoverished by inflation and by a deficit in the budget, weakened and subservient to large private interests, and tied to the civil and military bureaucracy. The reasons for this lay in the way in which domestic and economic policies had been carried out during the war:

politically the country had been harshly repressed, and economically the trend had been to hand over available resources to industrial enterprises, which supplanted the state and reduced it to the role of intermediary or customer.

The war meant that in all classes, in both town and country, wealth moved to the industrialists and to a few large businessmen; the new wealth of these businessmen in particular showed up the general impoverishment of the country. In the war years wage-earners were particularly hard hit, especially those in industry. After the war the majority of workers and some of the peasants (particularly in the Po valley, in Tuscany and in Umbria) longed for a revolution which would break the power of the bourgeoisie and put it into their hands instead. In 1919–20 a great many large strikes took place in both town and country, which resulted in a general increase in real hourly wages. The increase was particularly large in industry, yet the difference between wages in industry and in agriculture continued to be, as it had been during the war, less than it had been in 1913. This (together with an obvious increase in the number of small landowners) was one of the few permanent results of the upheavals which the war produced in the peasants' world.*

But although the situation does show some changes brought about by the war in the distribution of wages, it gives no indication of the state of mind of workers, peasants, and men working in the public services (particularly the railways) during 1919–20, the 'two red years'. The workers' most pressing problem, which justified their repeated strikes,

---

* Agricultural wages (as opposed to wages in kind) have in this context only a relative importance, since they constitute only a part – with payment concentrated in the Po valley – of the earnings of agricultural workers. However, they should be borne in mind, although with the proviso that they are only one indication of the material conditions of agricultural workers.

was how to make their nominal wages keep up with 'galloping' inflation. Admittedly there was a general air of well-being because of the lack of unemployment, due to deaths in the war and in the epidemic of Spanish flu, and emigration, which had begun again after the war. This very lack of unemployment increased the bargaining power of trade unionists and allowed workers successfully to fight the effects of inflation on their wages; particularly because inflation itself, until the middle of 1920, made the business world euphoric and persuaded industrialists to give higher wages.

Discontent in the country was a result, in particular, of the fact that the government had not kept the promises it had made during the war to hand over land to poor peasants. Men wished not so much to keep wages up as to improve their employment contracts, to fight traditional unemployment (with the tax on labour) and to seek to occupy uncultivated land. On the other hand the conditions of many mezzadri* (in the central areas) and small tenant farmers (in the north) were good; during the war, by struggling hard, they had managed to save, and in the twenties they bought land, thus becoming small landowners. This spontaneous, small-scale agrarian reform, which made up in a small way for the promises which the government had made during the war and had since broken, was one of the permanent effects of the war – and certainly the most important – upon the countryside.

Discontent reigned not only among workers and peasants, but among the bourgeoisie, and particularly among the intelligentsia. They had enthusiastically supported the war aims, both the democratic and the expansionist. It was particularly hard for these people to get back into civilian life. Many looked back nostalgically to the prestige they had enjoyed as officers, which was very much greater than any

*Sharecroppers. [Translator's note.]

they had as civilians. Many, either from idealism or from material need, had a profound longing for greater social justice. Like the socialists, they were outraged by the sight of war profiteers, the 'sharks' as they were called. But they hated the socialists, who had wounded them in their tenderest sensibilities: in their feelings as middle-class people and as ex-combatants. The sufferings they had undergone together in the trenches had not been enough to make them overcome their traditional detachment from – indeed, it might even be contempt for – the proletariat. The antagonism between *interventisti* and *disfattisti* was partly the antagonism between the middle classes and the proletariat.

All these motives, together with an often exaggerated patriotism, now meant that many middle-class people longed for a strong-arm policy. They were deeply disturbed by the conditions meted out to Italy in the peace treaties. They felt that the treachery of the Allies at the conference table had robbed them of the spoils of victory, and criticized harshly not only the Allies but the Italian parliament and government, which, they maintained, had failed to protect national interests, and all *renunciatori*.* Many were ready to turn this criticism into direct action against the legal authority of the state. The middle classes provided the main support first for D'Annunzio's exploits in Fiume, and later for fascism.

They had – apart from industrialists and businessmen – suffered economically through the war, as the wage-earners had done. Wage-earners had suffered more during the war itself, but after it, whereas wages on the whole increased, the average level of income for the whole population was slightly lower than it had been before the war. A similar situation could be seen in France; but in Italy it was more

* Specifically, though here a broader meaning is suggested, those who were prepared to give up Dalmatia, part of Istria and the Trieste hinterland in order to conciliate the Yugoslavs. [Translator's note.]

serious because the real income figures were very much lower. The slight increase which had taken place since pre-war days in the level of tariffs throughout the world struck the property-owning classes in particular.

To these economic and social difficulties were added others, political and parliamentary. The traditional political class was divided into ex-interventionists and ex-neutralists, led respectively by Nitti and Giolitti. The general election of 1919, in which proportional representation was used and the suffrage was more broadly based than it had been in 1913, had provided legal representation that corresponded more closely to the reality of life in Italy than it had done before, and had helped to upset further, indeed to make impossible, the old parliamentary majority; this election has, in fact, been called an electoral revolution.

There was a very strong Socialist Party fiercely in opposition. There was a strong new party, the Popular Party (*partito popolare*)*, which, although it supported the government, had taken an important part of its mass support from the traditional political class. Outside parliament, the country tossed restlessly between the futile revolutionary or subversive aspirations of the left and the right. A famous right-wing example of this was D'Annunzio's seizure of Fiume in September 1919, which meant that parliament was dealt a second blow – the first being the country's intervention in the war.

The most consistent effort to overcome the critical situation, while holding on to the liberal parliamentary régime, was that made by the elderly Giolitti, who returned for the last time as head of the government in 1920–21. In foreign policy, Giolitti and his Foreign Minister Sforza managed to

---

*The Catholic party founded after the First World War by Don Luigi Sturzo, a Sicilian priest. It was, in the Italian context, rather more left than right. [Translator's note.]

put an end to the occupation of Fiume at the end of 1920 and to find a satisfactory solution for the embittered problem of the Adriatic. In home affairs, Giolitti tried to follow two lines, which ought to have offset each other: on the one hand, he kept to a strictly conservative policy intended to strengthen the liberal ruling classes, and, by taking advantage of even the armed violence of the fascists, to put down the two great mass parties, the Popular Party and even more the Socialist Party, in order to bring the latter back to its pre-war collaboration with the industrialists and with the liberals; on the other hand he brought in an energetic reform of the tax laws in order to improve the disastrous state of the public finances and to make the rich, who had gained most benefit from it, pay at least a part of the economic cost of the war.

At first, these policies seemed to be yielding good results. In foreign affairs they had been successful, and during 1921 it seemed that the worst of the post-war crisis was over and that things were moving towards a solution. The country's budget had decidedly improved. The political split between ex-interventionists and ex-neutralists had been healed. The socialist masses were weary from the enormous efforts they had made in August and September of 1920, during which they occupied the factories, and had practically given up their attempts at revolution. Internationally, too, revolution had waned: while the factories were being occupied in Italy, the Red Army, having reached the outskirts of Warsaw, ceased to advance further west.

But to be successful Giolitti's policies needed an extended period of economic euphoria, which would make the rich (apart from the leaders of the iron and steel industry) accept the harsh taxation, even if they grumbled at it. And by the spring of 1921 the economic slump which had hit the rest of the world in 1920 and had in the autumn given obvious warnings of its arrival in Italy was added to the country's social and political troubles. This economic crisis, that is, the fall in prices, did have certain beneficial effects on the public finances in Italy, since it helped to check inflation and the deficit in the budget. But the workers paid for it in terms of wage claims and unemployment. Giolitti found it possible to abolish the politically-fixed price of bread, which helped a great deal to reduce the deficit in the state's budget, because the socialists were so much less aggressive than they had been. At the same time the crisis forced him to abandon his policies, because the rich, although they were given concessions, such as customs protection and a share in public expenditure (the provision of railway equipment), were no longer ready to accept his tax policy. In conclusion: in the autumn of 1920 there was a slackening of revolutionary fervour in Italy and a sense of renewal in the traditional ruling classes. But it was not Giolitti who benefited from this sense of renewal. In the autumn of 1920 fascism appeared on the political scene.

Benito Mussolini was born in Romagna; his father was working-class and a socialist, and he himself had been an ardent socialist. He had the virtues and even more the vices of the working-class man from Romagna – or rather, of the caricature of such a man. Impetuous by nature, he loved violence, yet was also easily frightened; occasionally he showed a certain sincere humanity and generosity, but this generosity consisted mainly of pride and vanity. In him, the socialist resentment of those in power was not so much a wish for justice as a wish for subversion as an end in itself; it was petty bourgeoisie's envy of, and sense of frustration towards, the rich. When he later achieved his goal and was the most powerful man of all, Mussolini retained some of the parvenu's snobbishness. He did not despise money, but was too ambitious to make it his main object in life. In spite of his love of violence, he avoided killings and crimes as far as possible (and in comparison with other dictators); this may have been due partly to his admitted humanity, but was probably due more to the fact that he rated the high political price of bloodshed at its true value. When this political price did not exist, he accepted murders and massacres quite calmly. During the war in Ethiopia in 1935–6 poison gas was used widely, and battles were fought with the object of annihilating the enemy, battles which did, indeed, end with the enemy being wiped out entirely. When the Abyssinian people began to rebel, after their defeat by fascist Italy, Mussolini himself gave chilling orders for mass murders.

He was a cunning corrupter of men, who could play on their faults whenever he had a chance to do so; the faults of the ordinary people, and those of men in power. He had no faith in people – indeed, he despised them. He had no friends. To the ordinary people he was always close, in the way that a party leader is close to his followers and, even more, in the way that an actor is close to the crowd of his admirers in the theatre.

Contrary to appearances, he was basically a weak man, often irresolute and changeable in making decisions. But when he was on form what seemed to be hesitancy was really his highest political quality, which showed him to be a great tactician: this was his capacity to wait, to act at the right moment, to get the maximum result from the minimum effort. The mask of strength behind which he hid answered only in part to the need to rule which often characterizes natures which appear authoritarian but are inwardly weak; above all, it answered to the needs of the party leader and of the actor.

He was almost a great journalist and, even politically, had the qualities and faults of the journalist: an acute capacity to diagnose the political situation, a very exact realization of what the public wanted, polemical ability, a sharp, lively and superficial intelligence, and the disorganized, rough-and-ready culture of a dilettante. The label that suits him best is that of a political adventurer, in the sense that until 1915 his moral and intellectual life was ruled by confusion; therefore, as the years went by, he came more and more to prefer personal success to any other consideration. He was a man ready for anything, including, in the first place, the subversion of Italian institutions, not in order to forward an idea but to forward his own personal success. During the twenty years of fascist rule fascism became an idea: Mussolini never considered himself as being at the service of this idea, but thought that the idea was there to serve his person.

Among the leaders of the socialist parties, Mussolini had been the most gifted revolutionary agitator. He had left the Socialist Party and joined the campaign which supported the war in 1914–15, maintaining that the coming war would have a revolutionary character. Immediately after the war, he appeared to be politically finished. The entire revolutionary or subversive section of the left and the right – his section – was taken over: on the left by the socialists, on the right by D'Annunzio and the nationalists. But Mussolini refused to accept defeat. The political situation was fluid. He had to start somewhere. One thing might always lead to another. His activity was ever a mixture of petty opportunism, which came to be called realism, and of a perhaps involuntary fidelity to certain directives that remained constant. This is one of the reasons why the twenty years of fascism, seen from a distance, appear to develop in a consistent way; but seen from close to, they appear as a continuous and almost chaotic series of changes of political direction.

On 23 March 1919, Mussolini and a few dozen followers founded the first 'Fascio di combattimento', or fascist fighting unit. The name was linked to the revolutionary fascists who had supported the war and to the parliamentary fascist group for national defence, founded after Caporetto. The movement intended to set itself up as the heir of the revolutionary syndicalist tradition, and of the nationalist tradition. It aimed in two directions: on the one hand, as its name suggested, it exploited the differences between ex-combatants and ex-neutralists, and claimed Fiume and Dalmatia for Italy; on the other, it stood as a left-wing movement, almost a rival of the Socialist Party. In reality, whatever Mussolini's confused intentions may have been in those early days, fascism was a right-wing movement, rivalling D'Annunzio and the nationalists. For this reason the Milanese upper-middle classes, although not excessively impressed by it, supported its emergence.

The movement had little success, and in the general elections of 1919 it was soundly defeated. Mussolini then felt it was opportune, without denying his left-wing slant, to emphasize the fact that he called himself a free-trader. Free trade was what the property-owning classes wanted; they wanted a policy which promoted industrial production and meant to free themselves from what they called the harness of war, which in particular meant high taxation and trade union bondage: high wages, collective bargaining, taxes on labour, etc. Mussolini's move was intended to strengthen or to gain the favour and support of these classes, while at the same time he did not give up trying to secure a broad basis of popular support.

In 1921 he stated as a matter of policy that fascism would take all economic content away from the state and fill it, instead, with a spiritual content. He went on to say that fascism in its original state was against parties, and for the trade unions. The working-class movement, Mussolini also said in 1921, echoing both the anxieties of property owners and, in a confused way, the general uneasiness in the world of labour and production, must take on new forms, unlike the old, outdated forms of the Socialist Party. Fascism was to be the synthesis between the indestructible ideas of the free market economy and these new forms of the working-class movement.

So long as the wealthy remained on the defensive, fascism was not even modestly successful. But from the autumn of 1920 (D'Annunzio was by then politically finished and his followers were going over to fascism), fascist strong-arm tactics were used more and more openly in the countryside of the Po valley, Emilia and Tuscany. These were the 'red' parts of the country, in which landowners and tenant farmers, large and small (including, in the forefront, the new small landowners who had come into being at the time), small tradesmen and shopkeepers, infuriated by the aggressiveness of the socialist organizations, counter-attacked as soon as the general change in political situation allowed them to do so.

The fascist action squads violently destroyed the socialist peasant leagues and co-operatives, and later those of the *popolari* as well. These squads consisted of young men from the bourgeoisie and petty bourgeoisie of the countryside and of provincial towns. Many were students, but some were socially humbler and there were working-class youngsters among them as well: a mixture of idealists, spoilt brats, misfits and hooligans. Some of them were demobilized officers or else sons or younger brothers of demobilized officers. They were all young, some very young, proud of their youth and of the war they had fought in or merely dreamed about, and in their violence they employed methods used by shock troops in the war. The life and dignity of others mattered little to them; indeed, it might even seem right and creditable to humiliate them.

Until then, fascism had been a small movement in the towns. From the end of 1920 it became preponderantly rural.

In the same period, from 1921 onwards, fascist trade unions began to take over from socialist trade unions and to spread throughout the country districts dominated by the fascist squads. The new forms of the working-class movement foretold by Mussolini had their origins in these trade unions which united the rural masses, working- and lower-middle-class. It was in the countryside, and not only among the urban petty bourgeoisie, that fascism found its basis of mass support.

In 1921, while the industrialists put their hopes in Giolitti rather than in fascism, the farms of the north and the big landowners of central Italy joined or supported fascism in a less ambiguous way. The reasons for this lay in the concessions which Giolitti had made to the industrialists (state protection and purchasing of railway equipment) and in the fact that farmers were going through a difficult time. The economic slump, where it was linked to the problems of labour, was a safety valve for the industrialists but a menace to the farmers. Indeed, unemployed workers who left the towns and returned to the countryside where they originally came from had to be employed by the farmers, who were weighed down by the tax on labour.

This was a time of conflict between industrialists and farmers. The industrialists were asking for an increase in customs duties. The farmers, on the other hand, were strictly free-traders, because, given the general situation, it was for the time being impossible to re-impose the duties which were in their favour – that is, those on corn and sugar, abolished during the war. The industrialists came out of the situation best; the farmers had to bear the brunt of things. As we shall see later, the traditional alliance between industrialists and farmers was not re-established until 1925, although, from 1922, their mutual opposition lessened. Once the economic slump had been overcome, once customs duties had been increased and international trading reorganized, both Confindustria* and the government again regarded the increase of exports as a fundamental factor in development. After 1922, the customs policy pursued was one of free trade, which satisfied the growers of market-garden produce and fruit for export. Those who suffered particularly from this policy were the large landowners and farmers who were tied to fixed incomes and to crops not meant for export, and the sugar-beet growers.

Not all industries were aiming to increase exports. There were firms closely linked to the banks and more interested in the increase of public spending, such as electrical firms, iron and steel firms, arms manufacturers and shipbuilding firms: all of which, with the very important exceptions of the electrical firms and of Fiat, had the greatest difficulty in adapting themselves to the peacetime economy and, with their monopoly of trade in their particular fields, were putting a brake upon the country's economic development. Indeed, the heavy capital accumulations of the banks took financial resources away from other firms, while public expenditure helped to increase costs and reduce exports. Even more serious were the effects of the high tariffs imposed in the twenty years between the two world wars by the electrical industry, for which the whole of domestic industry paid a heavy price, particularly during the Depression, and particularly the small and medium-sized industrial firms and Southern Italy. But, for all these negative aspects, the electrical firms had a direct interest in the development of the industry as whole and in the widening of the market, and, above all, most of them had a dynamic character that, once the post-war crisis was over, allowed them to go straight on to the open market and to free themselves

*Confederation of Italian Industry. [Translator's note.]

from the banks. The other large and most energetic firms, such as Montecatini, Snia Viscosa, Fiat and the major textile firms, made similar use of the open market and of their own possibilities of raising capital.

At the beginning, fascism had – quite apart from its left-wing tendency – connections with a sympathy for the large iron and steel industry, which seemed likely to suffer most from the ending of the war and which felt it was in its own interest to keep the country in a state of agitation. It has recently been proved that, in 1919–20, the Ilva steelworks financed *Il Popolo d'Italia*, and it is significant that, as far as one can see, this financing began in the summer of 1919, that is, at just the time when D'Annunzio was preparing for his exploits in Fiume. Both D'Annunzio and Mussolini were intended by their financial backers to be the means of maintaining disorder in the country and of dividing the mass movement.

But, as I have said, in 1920 and even more in 1921 Mussolini emphasized his faith in a liberal economic policy, interpreted as the restraining not so much of protectionism and public spending as of taxes, and as the destruction of the 'fetters' of war. When later, after the economic crisis of 1921, the two largest iron and steel firms – Ilva and Ansaldo – sank, the fascists, while protesting strongly against the government's indifference, in fact abandoned them. Free trade, linked to the request for particular intervention by the state to save this or that enfeebled firm, allowed Mussolini to make the fascist movement support, in a pliant kind of way, the complex and partly opposing aspirations of the wealthy classes, whether industrial or landowning.

Fascism was born in a set of economic circumstances in which the longing for protectionism and public spending, led by the iron and steel industry, was strong; but it made itself felt, and, even more, achieved power and carried it for-

ward substantially until 1931, in a set of economic circumstances in which the dominant wish was to restrain protectionism, high taxes and public expenditure. This does not
mean that from 1922 onwards and, even more, from 1925
onwards, protectionism, already high taxes and public expenditure did not continue to increase. But these increases
were generally considered a negative, even if necessary, fact;
they were not part of a consistent ideology either of Confindustria or – still less – among the civil servants at the economic ministries.

It must be added at once, however, that Mussolini always
tried to make fascism distinct from classic reaction; that is,
he always tried to keep a certain distance between fascism
and the bourgeoisie, and, in particular, its dominant groups,
and to barter with these groups advantages which he guaranteed them in order to make them accept in exchange – in
matters sometimes of foreign policy, sometimes of economic
policy – aspirations and directives which they did not always
like. In other words fascism, like parliamentary government,
aimed not to identify itself automatically with a single sector
of society, but to work as a political mediator between the
various sectors. There was, however, a special link with the
bourgeoisie because fascism, while suppressing the free development of working-class and trade union movements, was
very careful not to do the same – in spite of a few verbal
statements on the subject – to the economic activity of the
bourgeoisie.

In 1921, fascism spread not only in the country but in the
towns of northern and central Italy. Here, too, it found the
mainspring of its success in interests which had suffered, or
else in the rage and bitterness aroused by the socialists. Sometimes it was a bitterness which had roots far into the past,
and went back to the crisis of 1898–9, when the reactionaries
had been beaten by the forces of democracy. 'In fascism lies

the salvation of our freedom,' the fascists sang in the streets. They sang with their familiarly bold and often arrogant air. Not all respectable people approved of that air, but they all recognized their own feelings in the words of the song. In fascism they saw freedom from the fetters of war and high taxation, freedom from the high wages, strikes and indiscipline of the workers, freedom from the demands of workers' confederations and from the rivalry of co-operatives, freedom from the fear of revolution and from the irritating and overweening arrogance of the workers, freedom to make some use of the war they had fought and the victory they had won.

A young man of good family, son of a decent professional man and destined to follow in his father's footsteps, was one day walking through the streets of Turin when he met a group of workers. 'Take off your collar!' they shouted at him, eyeing him in a none too friendly manner. That was all. But from that moment the young man, who until then had watched the development of political events in a fairly indifferent way, became an ardent fascist. The incident is true; but it might well be invented, so typical is it of the situation and of the psychological reaction which it aroused.

In a few months the fascist movement had grown with the momentum of a landslide. In 1919 it had 17,000 members, in November 1921, 310,000. This success was due first of all to the situation I have just described. In the second place it was due to the liking felt by minor government officials for the fascist squads, and often to the help they gave them, in spite of the illegality of their actions. Even Giolitti indirectly favoured the fascists and their illegality, believing that he could later absorb them into the legal system. Whereas what actually happened was that the fascist movement and its illegal behaviour continued to grow. Giolitti's successor, Bonomi, made an effort, though with little success, to stand up to them more firmly.

At the end of 1921 the Italian working-class movement and its political and trade union organizations had, after a year of the fascist offensive, almost been swept away. The object of fascism began to be the achievement of power. In the same period – November – the fascist movement formed itself into a party. It was not always easy for Mussolini to dominate the movement and later the party as well, both movement and party having grown in such a fast, tumultuous and spontaneous way. The very spontaneity of fascism, although it gave it much of its vitality, also demonstrated its centrifugal and, in some ways, anarchical tendencies. Quite often cases occurred of local leaders – known as *ras** – refusing the discipline of the central organization. Both then and later there was a fair number of cases of idealistic fascists leaving the movement and the party because they were disgusted by what they thought to be the betrayal of its early programme.

On the whole, Mussolini managed to manoeuvre cleverly, showing remarkable opportunism and tactical sense, concentrating or trying to concentrate his fire on those who were becoming or seemed to be the institutions which bore up the liberal state. The traditional political class had viewed fascism favourably, and continued to do so, insofar as it was weakening or destroying the Socialist Party and the organizations of the working-class movement; but it watched with growing anxiety the illegal aspects of fascism, to which there was now almost no point, since the Socialist Party was half destroyed. Mussolini used legal and illegal weapons at the same time: both parliament and the fascist squads. With the first he reassured people, with the second he struck at them. However, it would not be entirely true to say that he used

* A word of Ethiopian origin, meaning 'strong local chieftain'. [Translator's note.]

legal methods only to hide his illegal methods. He used both and, on the whole, tended to put a brake upon the subversive tendencies of the squads and some of the *ras*. This helped, among other things, to make him appear to traditional politicians the one man capable of channelling fascism into legality.

The conservatives' wish for legality (sincere while at the same time more or less hypocritical) was mingled with another, profounder wish which is the key to an understanding of why fascism was able to achieve power even when the situation of post-war crisis and revolutionary danger which had justified its success at the beginning no longer existed. This was the wish of conservatives and of the bourgeoisie to halt the advance of democracy which had occurred since the war and to restore the old balance between the ruling classes and the mass of the people. In order to achieve this, they had to suppress the challenge of working-class parties, lower the level of wages, and restore total freedom to the entrepreneurs by abolishing the controls and attempts at control which had been introduced in those years (in particular, factory grievance committees, restrictive practices and the tax on labour in the country).

Mussolini's tactics were wholly successful. During 1922, in spite of improved economic conditions, the instability of the government and the lack of will-power among those in charge reached their height. This was not entirely a result of the threat of fascist illegal action. In order to defuse this illegality, it seemed increasingly necessary for fascism to be asked to share the responsibilities of government. In October Mussolini was offered the chance of taking part, with some of his followers, in a new government, over which Giolitti would preside, or else Facta (the Prime Minister), or else Salandra. Mussolini, now in a strong position because he was supported by the most prominent members of the Milanese upper-middle class, finally refused. In spite of his small following in parliament, he felt he could now expect more. He would form the government himself. This was the reason for the March on Rome.

With the exception of the communists and nearly all the socialists, the whole of parliament, including the democratic anti-fascists and the socialists of the CGL (Confederazione Generale del Lavoro), welcomed Mussolini's government with a sigh of relief, as the end of a nightmare. The civil war, people said, was over; fascism would, it was hoped, at last behave legally.

The March on Rome, like the intervention of 1915, was a show of strength against a parliamentary majority. This show of strength would have failed if the king had opposed it. But, as in 1915, the king felt it was right not to oppose it. He had little faith in parliament, feared the socialists, and – as a good anticlerical – hated the popular party. As a person, the bourgeois, unrhetorical monarch hardly seemed the kind of man to get on well with Mussolini. But he was afraid to make an enemy of him: until shortly before, Mussolini had been a republican; the ambitious Duke of Aosta was notoriously pro-fascist and the danger could not be discounted that he might take over the throne of his cousin Victor Emmanuel. In the months and years before this the king had discounted the possibility of a military dictatorship and had finally pinned all his hopes on the ageing Giolitti. When Giolitti failed, the solution offered by Mussolini seemed to him the one that might best be able to bring order and settled conditions to the country in its quarrelling post-war state; as the two traditional enemies of the liberal state – the priests and the socialists – would never be able to do.

2

FASCISM IN POWER

MUSSOLINI began his career as Prime Minister through the method, which was by then familiar in him, of blowing hot and cold. He goaded and insulted the Chamber of Deputies in a famous speech 'from the bivouac',* yet was careful to soften the meaning of that speech immediately after making it. In his request for full powers and in forming his government he followed strictly legal and traditional criteria. He formed a cabinet that leaned towards the right and the centre, with fascists, *popolari*, democrats, liberals and nationalists taking part. There was even an attempt – which failed – to get the participation of a socialist of the CGL. The participation of the Popular Party was most encouraged, after that of the fascists. Apart from the greater number of fascists, it was a government substantially similar to that which Giolitti, among others, had hoped to be able to form in the previous months.

During the first two months of his government, Mussolini managed to keep things legal (in spite of serious incidents provoked by the fascists in Turin). Internally, it was a matter of reassuring wealthy, respectable people that fascism in power, in spite of its aggressive attitudes, was a guarantee of order and the preservation of things as they were. The prob-

---

*The name commonly given to the speech of 16 November 1922 in which Mussolini addressed the Chamber for the first time as Prime Minister. The speech included this sentence: 'I could have turned this dim and dreary hall into a bivouac for platoons.' The Italian reads: 'Potevo fare da questa aula sorda o grigia un bivacco dei manipoli.' [Translator's note.]

lem, with regard to foreign powers, was similar, though more serious. Here, especially in the governments of the Allies, fascism's rise to power had caused some puzzlement and anxiety : people remembered what had seemed the wild, unbridled plans put forward many times by fascism with regard to foreign policy. Mussolini immediately gave special attention to foreign policy, which he took into his own hands; and behaved extremely cautiously. Besides, the news that fascism had achieved power had sent Italian share prices up at once on the main foreign stock-markets.

The first turns of the screw, cleverly spaced out in time, took place in January 1923 with the institution (prepared months earlier) of two party organs which had until then been unknown in the liberal state : the fascist militia and the fascist Grand Council. The first rounded up, disciplined and gave an appearance of legality to the disbanded fascist action squads; the second was intended to be the major organ of the fascist party and at the same time the link between the party and the government.

In February the freemasons were expelled from the fascist party and in March it merged with the nationalists. This meant that the obviously right-wing outlook which the party had been showing for some time was officially confirmed, as well as the influence of the nationalistic ideology which it had felt, in particular, through Alfredo Rocco. At the same time an article by Mussolini in his own publication *Gerarchia* made it clear that, having defeated socialism, fascism was now anxious to fight the anti-fascist liberals.

In April the *popolari* were thrown out of the government. From then onwards Mussolini managed, with growing success, to secure the support of the Vatican, which finally abandoned the Popular Party. The right-wing elements in this party gradually joined the fascists. The rescue operation undertaken on behalf of the Banco di Roma, which was linked to the Vatican's financial interests, must be seen as part of Mussolini's policy towards the Vatican and Catholic interests.

After a pause during May (due, among other things, to a visit to Rome by members of the British royal family) came what was, politically, a very hot summer. In June and July the Acerbo bill for electoral reform was presented and debated in parliament. Mussolini followed his usual line of strength and sweetness together. The presentation and debate of the Acerbo plan was, partly at the king's request, formally correct. Mussolini made some moderate and conciliatory statements. But the contents of the plan under discussion, weighted to benefit the majority, was designed to combat and put down in the sternest way all the political forces – socialist, popular and democratic – which did not support fascism and the government. Basically the Acerbo reform was the conservatives' reply to the 'electoral revolution' of 1919 (following on the unsuccessful reply in the elections of 1921), and at the same time it was the means by which Mussolini's régime – which has been called 'the authoritarian and personal régime of a political opportunist' – formally carried on until 3 January 1925. The conservative nature of this régime might recall some similar objectives in Giolitti's last government; but it differed clearly from that in its authoritarian aspects – which were fundamentally important – and in the absense of any ideas of reform.

After the debate on electoral reform, relations between the government and the bourgeois opposition became more strained. At the same time the Vatican showed its pro-fascist sympathies more clearly. A government circular, not put into effect at the time, gave prefects a very great deal of power over the freedom of the press. Mussolini's policy of moderation, which up to this time had characterized his foreign policy, was abruptly interrupted by the incident in Corfu, a sensational example of his diplomacy. He meant to carry out a spectacular formal annexation of the Dodecannese, with obviously anti-Greek, and implicitly anti-British, intentions. The unexpected massacre of the Italian mission under the command of General Tellini fell in with his intentions like a lighted match into petrol. The island of Corfu was occupied. Mussolini hoped to be able to change occupation into annexation, but Britain's firm stand dissuaded him.

During the period of the elections, up to a few days before they took place, Mussolini's tactics were to use force and illegality. Many local and provincial councils, in which the fascists were in a minority, were dissolved by the government. All working-class associations were placed under the surveillance of the prefects. A large number of incidents took place during the elections. The result of these elections, which were held in April 1924, was a victory for the government candidates, although with a smaller majority than had been expected. Thanks in particular to the socialists, the government was beaten in most of the north, but had a sensational success in the south.

Once the elections were over, Mussolini took up his double policy of toughness and gentleness. The Popular Party, now without the support of the Vatican, was in practice beaten. Having cleverly eliminated the communists and the extreme socialists, Mussolini now had to overcome the opposition of the constitutionalists under Giovanni Amedola, and that of the Reformist Socialists (*socialisti unitari*): the bulk of the legal opposition, that is.

In parliament Mussolini spoke brilliantly, cleverly, moderately. He asked his enemies to collaborate with him or else to oppose him in a considered, constructive way. What he could not accept – he said – was opposition on principle. Against

31

opposition of this kind Cesarino Rossi, who was then working closely with Mussolini at the Viminale,* had published
a threatening statement in the press. The constitutional and
Reformist Socialist opposition stood firm on their position of
principle. A few days later the unexpected, tragic scandal of
Giacomo Matteotti's murder broke out.

Once in power, Mussolini centralized the party and imposed discipline upon the ras and their followers. Violence
was allowed much less than it had been before and rarely
occured. On the other hand, his subordinates at the Viminale
had formed a secret group whose object was the undertaking
of acts of violence on orders, direct or indirect, from Mussolini
himself. Its enemies later called this group the fascist Cheka.
Important members of it were Rossi and, on the executive
side, a one-time squad member, the Tuscan Amerigo Dumini.

This so-called Cheka attacked two dissident fascists, Cesare
Forni and Alfredo Misuri, as well as Amendola and the Reformist Socialist Matteotti. These attacks were made on op-
ponents who, at that particular time, were giving Mussolini
most trouble. The victims were not killed, at least not immediately. Severe beatings and other acts of violence were
used to weaken their resistance, both moral and physical.
Certainly as far as Matteotti was concerned particularly
tough measures were planned, including imprisonment for a
while. It is not known how far they were prepared to go
before killing him. He was picked up in Rome by a closed car,
and as he struggled and shouted his kidnappers were afraid
of being caught red-handed and killed him.

The murder aroused great anger in Rome and other cities.
The widespread sympathy which fascism had aroused diminished or melted away, and in the week that followed the
crime the government might easily have been toppled. Mussolini was frightened. Luckily for him, none of his oppon-

*The Ministry of the Interior. [Translator's note.]

ents was up to the situation. All they did was walk out of the Chamber as a protest and later, with the exception of the communist deputies, produce what was known as the Aventine Secession. Mussolini got the situation in hand again, and, thanks to the persistent support of the fascist country districts, kept it so.

The situation was profoundly different, however, from what it had been before the murder, and remained uncertain during the whole of the second half of 1924. At the end of the year, things seemed to grow worse. In the face of increasing aggressiveness from the Aventine opposition, led by Amendola, and from the republican old-soldiers' association known as 'Italia libera', Mussolini, after a long, cautious wait, was forced to use a clear policy of force and illegal action. This was at last announced publicly, with perfect timing, on 3 January 1925. The king would have preferred to avoid it, but did nothing to oppose it.

Until Matteotti's murder Mussolini's plan had not been to establish what later came to be called the totalitarian fascist state. Officially and formally his plan was a restoration of the constitutional state; in fact, however, it was the establishment of his own authoritarian and personal régime, as a political opportunist. The main tool to hand to consolidate this régime was, on the political plane, the collaboration of those who were known as his supporters, led by the liberals; and, on the economic plane, the collaboration of the rich. The liberals supported the fascist government above all because they were afraid that if it fell the communists and socialists would return in strength. Immediately after the elections of April 1924 and before the Matteotti murder in May, Mussolini had secretly had another electoral reform prepared (through which Italy became one constituency) to consolidate his power at new elections in the future. On 3 January 1925 he also used this weapon, as well as that of force:

the Chamber gave way both to his forceful attitude and to the threat of new elections. The majority of liberal supporters supported fascism; a minority went over to the opposition.

From the economic point of view the period 1922–5 was on the whole, throughout the world and in Italy, clearly a time of revival and later of prosperity. In Italy the *per capita* income was higher than it had been before the war. In the early post-war years the taxes levied, which had reached their height in the autumn of 1920 through Giolitti's efforts, had been intended to produce more revenue and to weigh in particular upon the rich. In 1921–2 a reaction against this took place. The economic policy of the fascist government was under the direction of a free-trader, Alberto De Stefani, who gave a stimulus to the tax policy introduced in the previous two years, a policy intended to restore the traditional distribution, altered during the war and the post-war period, of taxes and revenue in order to favour the accumulation of capital and investments. It was a policy which strengthened the budget balance and helped the prosperous, productive classes. Taxes as a whole were increased, and direct taxation in particular went up. In spite of these direct taxes, the tendency increased to lighten fiscal pressure on capital, especially in the form of property. The increased fiscal burden (this was to last throughout the whole of the twenty years of fascism) weighed most heavily on land, therefore on the south. But the big decrease in estate duty favoured all property owners without distinction.

Real wages on the land (for men) went up and down: in 1922–3 they increased, going back almost to the level of 1920; in 1924 they went down and in 1925 they improved a little. Real industrial wages fell, emphasizing the tendency which had already shown itself in 1921. Besides this, the wages of state employees and employees in organizations subsidized by the state were subject to tax.

A few days after the formation of his government Mussolini withdrew the act passed by Giolitti on the registration of stock (disliked by the Vatican), and decided to put the telephone service into private hands, not to continue with the report of the inquiry on war expenses, and to give up the state monopoly on life assurance. Later the match industry was put into private hands. The large manufacturers, who ran the very powerful Confindustria, urged the government to concentrate its benevolence upon them, without spreading it to their weaker colleagues. But they were finally disappointed in De Stefani, not only and not so much because of his free-trading as because in March 1925 he took some measures to curb inflation which made trouble for industrial investments.

What had happened was that as late as 1925 the results of the war, the break which it had brought about in traditional balances, were still making themselves sharply felt on the economic and social level. The years 1922–5 were a period of transition not only politically (the installation of an authoritarian régime which, even on paper, was not yet totalitarian), but economically and socially. As we have seen, the agreement between industrialists and landowners, that is, the characteristic power bloc of the Italian state, had been broken after the war. Admittedly the agreement had been re-established in 1922, at least partly; but free trade damaged the absentee landlords and large-scale farmers, while favouring the small and medium-sized ones, who produced food for export. The period was characterized by an unusual vitality among small-holders but also by other factors: the need to carry forward economic post-war reconversion in an energetic way, which meant restraining the iron and steel, shipbuilding and armaments industries, in other words those most closely connected with public spending; and the opposition between the interests of large-scale trading with the outside world, particularly in Trieste, and the interests of industry.

All this ceased in 1925 with the appointment of Volpi as Minister of Finance in succession to De Stefani. Steps were taken in favour of industrial investments; the restoration and increase of customs duties, including one on grain, and the revaluation of the lira, weighed upon the small-holder to the advantage of the large landowner, and successfully re-established the protectionist bloc between industrialists and landowners. However, the damage done to this bloc by the consequences of the war was so great that it had difficulty in working in its characteristic, traditional form, and was always on the point of breaking up again during the Depression in the thirties. Two points must be made, however. The first is that after 1925 the bloc was held together not so much by protectionism as by the financial interchange of industrial capital and landed capital (both urban and country). The second is that the control of the working classes by the property-owning classes was thus assured, not only by the bloc but above all, thanks to fascism, by a freezing of socially dynamic ideas, to which we shall return in the next chapter.

Shortly after the restoration of protectionism on corn, in 1928–30 the industrialists and the Banca Commerciale joined together and took over the shipbuilding and trade interests in Trieste. The years 1922–5 had been a period of relative fluidity, which had been stimulated by inflationary boosts; the years 1925–9 were a period in which the old balances, even more closely controlled by finance capital, were fully restored and consolidated. As we shall see, on the political level, too, the period 1925–9 was one of consolidation and decisive development for the fascist régime.

In 1922–5 another area of friction between industry and the government was that of the trade unions, where fascism was particularly sensitive because it hoped to gain the support of the working classes. Fascist trade unionists, under the leadership of Edmondo Rossoni, aimed for what was called integral trade unionism, that is, they sought to include within a single organization all those who gave men work and all those who did this work. Landowners and agricultural wage-earners were prepared to accept this plan : partly, and perhaps above all, because they had less power, but also because fascist trade unionism was prevalent in the countryside, where the class war had, by then, been suppressed. Whereas the industrialists successfully opposed Rossoni's plan, and it was dropped.

At the end of 1923 Mussolini told the industrialists, gathered around him in the Palazzo Chigi, that capital and labour ought not to quarrel, but to collaborate; that the government would guarantee order (even the holiday on 1 May had been abolished) but in exchange the industrialists must raise wages, which were high enough in the countryside but too low in industry. The request for wage increases was further justified by the fact that prices had been rising and in 1925–6 this had turned into real inflation. As industrial wages had not risen, indeed were dropping, in the summer of 1924 and even more in March 1925 there were strikes promoted by the fascist trade unions. At the end of 1925 the industrialists tried to escape the jurisdiction of the newly-appointed official Labour Board. The Minister of Justice Alfredo Rocco, a former nationalist, favoured their request and the idea of placing only the country workers under the Labour Board. But Mussolini opposed the idea and this time the industrialists had to give way.

These conflicts checked and limited but did not impede Mussolini in his efforts to make the Italian state fascist, as we shall see in the next chapter.

3

THE FASCIST STATE

MUSSOLINI'S speech on 3 January 1925 opened up a new period in the history of Italy. People continued to talk about the restoration of the *Statuto** but in fact from then onwards it was not a matter of restoring the *Statuto* but, as was said later, of going beyond it. Italy was no longer a liberal state. It was aiming to become a fascist state, the first of the fascist states. The move from the liberal to the fascist state, in institutions and in laws, began during 1925, was completed in the next two years, and was crowned in 1929 by the Concordat and the plebiscite.

Freedom of the press was suppressed, in practice, during 1925. Between January of that year and the end of 1926 other laws were put forward and approved : freemasonry was suppressed; the government was given very wide powers to make legal decrees; the legal codes were reformed; the civil service was 'made fascist'; the person of the head of the government became superior to that of other ministers, and became independent of the legislative power and responsible only to the crown (the analogy with the figure of the German-style chancellor was more apparent than real); citizenship was taken away from political exiles, and sometimes their goods as well; the autonomy of local councils was restricted, and then suppressed. Finally the death penalty was introduced and a special court set up to deal with crimes against the security of the state, that is, against the fascist régime.

*The *Statuto Albertino*, the liberal constitution of 1848, which set up a parliamentary democracy. [Translator's note.]

The originators of all these laws, which were known as the 'highly fascist' laws, were two former nationalists: Luigi Federzoni, in his role as Minister of the Interior, and, above all, the Minister of Justice Rocco.

Mussolini carried this complex operation through successfully. He was helped by the fact that, owing to the economic prosperity at the time, fascism was generally popular throughout the country, at least until the end of 1926. Besides, he behaved with his usual shrewdness, once more using both the pressures of fascist extremism, and the curb of respectable opinion.

Until Matteotti's murder the Ministry of the Interior – the key ministry in controlling the country – had been under Mussolini's personal direction. After Matteotti's murder he handed it over to Federzoni, who until then had been Minister of the Colonies. Federzoni was a conservative, a monarchist, a man on the side of order: in other words, a guarantee to all those who, although they hated the opposition, had been shaken by the Matteotti crime and were afraid of fascist extremism – of what were known as 'leaps in the dark'. Federzoni was dismissed from the Ministry of the Interior in 1926, when the state had been irrevocably 'made fascist'. His presence there was an excellent way of covering the undermining of liberal institutions, and of guaranteeing the conservative character of the operation.

In the same period the direction of the fascist party was given to two extremists: first to Francesco Giunta, and then, in February 1925, to Roberto Farinacci, who was the most authoritative and the most ruthless of the fascist *ras*. Mussolini did not like him. With him and with Giunta he often used an energetic tone in order to restrain their impatience and their intemperate feelings. But both men were useful to him, and he used them. He gave way, as far as he felt was suitable, to their wish to 'make the state fascist', which often meant merely getting rid of officials thought to be anti-fascist. In this way, Mussolini also gave vent to his followers' longing for conquest ('To whom does Italy belong?' 'To us!').

Farinacci, like Federzoni, was dismissed from his job during 1926. Differences and conflicts often arose between state officials and party officials; in the countryside particularly, where the prefect often quarrelled with the fascist *federale*.* Later there were similar conflicts between high officials in the party and the under-secretary for the Interior or the Chief of Police. Mussolini always preferred to support state officials against party officials. In these early years it was quite clear where his support lay: a circular of 5 January 1927 established the superiority of the prefect to the *federale*. The state, it was said, was superior to the party. This had been the wish of the ex-Minister of the Interior, Federzoni.

One of the reasons for Mussolini's success continued to lie in his sense of what was suitable, which made him appear as the party's moderate. On the other hand, he was careful not to dissolve the party into the state, as some people would have liked him to do. The party and the militia were weapons held in reserve, to be kept in the background or rattled in the foreground, depending on the circumstances. Mussolini himself, in his Augusteo speech on 22 June 1925, had loudly proclaimed fascism's totalitarian and imperial will, and the need to 'make Italy fascist'. This was then taking place and the speech of 22 June invigorated the process. However, the chance of subordinating the party to the state – which Mussolini strongly supported in order to gain the sympathy of conservatives – in the long run helped to weaken the party itself, which indeed, during the thirties, finally melted into the state and almost disappeared as an autonomous political force.

In the same period in which he made the Augusteo speech,

* The provincial secretary of the fascist party. [Translator's note.]

Mussolini was giving his diplomatic representative abroad directives (preceding the later laws on political exiles) which meant that Nitti's Italian citizenship was in practice taken away from him. Nitti was then the most famous of the exiles and the one watched most carefully by Mussolini. Some weeks later, Amendola suffered an attack, from which he later died. He was a southern Italian, strong, austere and noble, a character of tragic seriousness both by vocation and from necessity. For this character, he paid with his death. A similar fate was later that of a young and even more intransigent intellectual from Turin, Piero Gobetti.

The opposition, the Aventine Secession, fell wretchedly apart. Those who were willing to make an act of submission could get back into the Chamber: Mussolini never refused anyone who submitted. The others were expelled from the Chamber in November 1926 and became exiles, either at home or abroad. In the same month, with Tito Zaniboni's attempt on Mussolini's life, the setting up of the special tribunal and the expulsion from the Chamber of the anti-fascist deputies, the last remains of free political argument were removed in Italy. Only in the Senate did a small group of liberals in opposition remain, faithful to the pre-fascist state. Among them were Benedetto Croce, Francesco Ruffini and the one-time editor of the *Corriere della Sera*, Luigi Albertini.

Until 1925 Mussolini had allowed the communists some freedom. It was good policy occasionally to wave the red rag of the 'Bolshevik peril' at the Italian middle classes, particularly in the Senate, and at the same time to let the Aventine opposition and communist opposition quarrel with each other. When the Aventine opposition collapsed, communist opposition was suppressed as well. Many communists were tried and imprisoned. Their leader, Antonio Gramsci, died after eleven years in detention.

The names mentioned here are the most famous. There were others, the unknown names of modest, simple men who suffered persecution and prison, who emigrated or who lived on in Italy as exiles.

It was more difficult, as we have seen, to make the relations between industrialists and workers bow to the new fascist law. The working classes in the north were anti-fascist, and the industrialists were traditionally hostile to state interference in their relations with their workers.

One of the fundamental principles of fascism was the collaboration between capital and labour. But ideas on the subject were very confused. This collaboration was sometimes known as syndicalism, sometimes as corporativism. As the industrialists were opposed to it, complete syndicalism was put aside and conflict between the classes was officially stated to exist; this conflict (it was said) would be settled in a higher synthesis by fascism.

Indeed, in June 1925 (at the same time as the Augusteo speech and almost at the time that protectionism was reintroduced) the Italian trade union movement was 'made fascist': the Grand Council decided that only fascist trade unions could represent the workers in bargaining with employers. On 2 October the fascist trade unionists and the industrialists came to an agreement of fundamental importance (the Palazzo Vidoni pact), pledging themselves to collaborate. On the fascist trade unionist side, collaboration meant giving up strikes and factory committees. To the industrialists, this was a great fundamental success, one that would, in spite of some resistance, make them yield to the government's request for juridical discipline to be imposed upon labour relations. In November 1925, the bill was first discussed, and in the first months of 1926 the government conceded another favour to the industrialists (dictated, however, by other considerations): it guaranteed them public supply contracts even if prices of products rose more than 5 per cent (the margin kept to until then) above those for the products of similar industries abroad.

Thus the important law of April 1926 was arrived at. It was fundamental on two points: it formally confirmed the renunciation of strikes and factory committees by trade unionists, and it extended collective contracts to all labour relations. The first of these two points favoured the industrialists, the second the workers. However, the first point was obeyed with a strictness never observed in dealing with the second. *Il Lavoro Fascista*, mouthpiece of the workers' unions, during the twenty years of fascism often pointed out how the employers had failed to observe the law. Besides this, the tendency was for collective contracts to be based on wages paid in the least efficient firms, that is, on the lowest wages.

Yet, in the short term, the law came at a time when the workers were doing well. Although official statistics do not confirm it, it seems that in the first half of 1926 real wages increased, thanks to the efforts of the fascist trade unionists; indeed in some cases they went back to the level of 1921–2.

Collaboration between capital and labour was not merely a case of doing what was necessary at a particular moment, that is, responding to the need to check and control the claims of the workers, whose wages were affected by the inflationary situation at the time. It was an answer to much more profound demands. As was said over and over again, it was a case of involving the mass of the people in the state. The roots of the problem went down, in particular, to the anti-Giolitti political thinking of the first fifteen years of the century. The problem had grown during the war years and had exploded dramatically after the war. The Italian ruling class was incapable of solving the problem with the traditional methods of a free society. Fascism was the answer to the problem. And indeed one of the characteristics peculiar to fascism, and not present in other reactionary movements, was the fact that trade unions did have a place in it and it did have a foundation of mass support.

On 21 April 1927, the Carta del Lavoro was promulgated. This was a series of general principles, the form of which showed ways in which capital and labour could collaborate, and the substance of which confirmed the rigid, organic subordination of labour to capital. The Carta stated that labour, whether executive or subordinate, intellectual or manual, was in the care of the state. It then went on to say that private enterprise was the most efficient and useful productive tool working in the interest of the nation, and that the state would intervene only when private enterprises failed or proved inadequate or when the interests of the state were involved. The Labour Board, which began to function in the same year, 1927, undertook to reduce wages, by getting them into line with the revaluation of the lira, and to control the lira's movements.

In 1928 fascist trade unionism, which until then had been predominantly rural, at last managed to enter the ranks of the urban proletariat. The fascist trade unions' success with the working class should be seen in relation to the increase in unemployment as a result of the revaluation of the lira, and above all as a result of the fact that in order to find a job it was in practice necessary to belong to a fascist trade union.

Once the working-class organizations had been 'made fascist', Mussolini agreed to a request from the industrialists. Under the regulation of 1 July 1926, which followed the law of 3 April of the same year, on the ordering of relations with labour, all the workers' unions were combined into a single Confederazione nazionale dei sindacati fascisti dei lavoratori (National Confederation of Fascist Unions), placed under

the presidency of Rossoni. It was an event of great importance for the forces of labour, who at last saw the restoration
of one confederated trade union. Mussolini allowed Rossoni
to take whatever stand he liked in order to gain the favour
of the working classes. The employers, on the other hand,
looked askance at what Rossoni was doing and disliked the
confederated union, and in 1928 they managed to make Mussolini dismiss Rossoni and dissolve the confederation, which
was divided into six autonomous confederations, each independent of the others, and corresponding to the employers'
six confederations.

It was said that this was a further step towards corporativism; which, as we shall see, was in a way true. But it seems
more accurate to say that it was intended to weaken the con-
tractual power of the workers' unions.

It is not unlikely that the dissolving of the confederated
union was decided by Mussolini in order, among other reasons, to overcome the perplexity of conservatives, chief among
them the industrialists, and the resistance they were putting
up to the state being made still more fascist. Conservatives
and industrialists feared that a complete reform of the state
in terms of fascism – that is, in terms of trade unionism and
corporativism, as far as labour relations were concerned –
would cut into the belief in private enterprise which had
been and still was the foundation of the government's economic policy. Some felt that, in order to guarantee these
private financial interests, it was best not to abolish entirely
some aspects of the liberal state.

Private financial interests were not touched. But the reform of the state was taken another definitive step forward in
1927–8, in the fundamental matter of political representation
and the legislative assembly.

Ideas on all this were confused, but some interesting points
did emerge. The theorists of corporativism, chief among them

the young Giuseppe Bottai, took as their point of departure the failure of the liberal state in the post-war crisis. What they criticized above all in the liberal state was the rift between political representation and the forces of production and labour, the entrepreneurs and the workers. The problem was to cure this split, to create a new type of political representation which would cling in a supple way to the forces of production and to those of labour, and, at the same time, to create a new type of relationship between employers and workers. This was what the theorists said.

As early as October 1925, the Grand Council had considered this question. In those days fascism still allowed, if only in theory, more than one party to exist. A solution had been put forward (it had, indeed, been put forward earlier, in 1910–11 and in 1919) which modified the principle of traditional political representation (entrusted to the Chamber) and the principle of labour representation: the Senate would be composed partly of representatives of the trade unions or corporations (the two words were still used interchangeably).

But nothing was done about it, either because in the next two years the true character of fascism appeared quite clearly when the other parties were suppressed, or else to avoid upsetting the king by taking part of the nomination of senators away from him. However, in 1928 the king and Mussolini came into conflict over the competence given to the Grand Council in the matter of the royal succession. Indeed, this provision was aiming, although quite gently, at restricting the freedom of the crown.

The Senate was still to be appointed by the king. Traditional political representation was suppressed and the Chamber was composed of representatives of the trade unions or corporations, who were confined to putting forward candidates, from among whom the Grand Council later selected a list to be submitted to the electors. The secret ballot was in practice abolished. The elections (Mussolini liked to emphasize, in a peculiarly fascist way, how much they irritated him) were called plebiscites.

Ten years later the Chamber, which was trade unionist and corporative only in name, underwent another reform. All signs of its being elected – even formal signs – disappeared. It was called *Camera dei fasci e delle corporazioni* (Chamber of the Fasces and Corporations) and was made up of representatives of the party's national council and of the corporations' national council, which had been set up in the meantime.

The first 'plebiscite elections', held in March 1929 as the climax of the building of the fascist state, were clearly a success for the régime. Perhaps the reason for this lay in another success – a great success – which Mussolini had achieved a month earlier: the Concordat.

Reconciliation with the Church and an end to the 'Roman question' had been sought by Mussolini for a number of reasons. With the Church's support, he hoped to induce the masses to enter fully into the fascist state, and, even more, to hold back the emancipation of the rural proletariat. The collaboration between the classes, imposed by fascism, which was coming to be called corporativism, had an exact precedent – although with important differences – in Catholic corporativism. But there were two other reasons, at least as important as this, which urged Mussolini along the way to the Concordat: first, he wanted to strengthen the prestige of fascism, and his own personal prestige, by cashing in on what had already been done by previous governments; and secondly, he wanted to exploit the Church's support by using it as a means of national expansion. Mussolini had admitted this latter motive in public as early as 1921, following on the nationalists' predictions.

As an ex-socialist from the Romagna, Mussolini had been strongly anti-clerical. His ecclesiastical policy and his wish to exploit religion as *instrumentum regni* were so open-minded that they could be called cynical; none of his predecessors in the government would have dreamed of such a thing. The king, being anti-clerical and representing tradition, had from the start been opposed to the idea of the Concordat. This open-mindedness was something new, a typical touch brought by Mussolini and fascism into Italian ecclesiastical policy.

It was a problem full of historical precedents. These had begun with Gioberti's myth of Italian supremacy and consisted of the tendency, supported several times by Catholic conservatives, liberals and nationalists, to use religion as a means of directing the working-class masses and of establishing national expansion, in the wake of the Pope's universal appeal. Sometimes – not always – it was not merely a narrow application of religion as *instrumentum regni*, but, in varying degrees, a matter of a sincere religious spirit. As the years went by this spirit weakened and the first motive took precedence over it.

Mussolini's ecclesiastical policy had links with the general post-war policy. While the tendency in ecclesiastical policy before the war had been to separate Church and state, the tendency after the war, in all countries, was to aim for a closer understanding with the Church. The times were critical, and the origins of this lay in the Russian Revolution and the fear of communism; it was therefore thought wise to seek the Church's support. And the Church, for its part, was now finding new connections with the financial and middle-class world, in place of its traditional connection with the world of landowners.

The policy of the Concordat, already set on its way by

Benedict XV, was viewed with special favour by Pius XI. Unlike his predecessor, Pius XI had an idea of Catholicism and of its relations with civil society which might be termed intransigent, theocratic and totalitarian. He believed that his instruments for implementing this idea should be the policy of the Concordat and Catholic Action.* He hated socialism and communism, and, although he deplored its excesses, he felt sympathetic towards fascism because it was illiberal and also because he saw it as a barrier against bolshevism. As I have said, during 1923 the Vatican abandoned the Popular Party and gradually came closer to fascism. Apart from all these motives, the Pope was also led to agree to the Lateran Pact in order to solve the financial difficulties which were besetting the Holy See.

But Mussolini had not come to the Concordat merely because his political ideas allowed him to take no notice of the principles which the liberal state had followed in its dealings with the Church. He knew that, thanks to the totalitarianism of the fascist régime, he could easily check any future theocratic aspirations on the part of the Church, and any clerical interference. In Mussolini's plans, the Concordat must see that the Church was strictly subordinated to the interests of the state. The Pope, of course, saw things in a different way.

Shortly after the signing of the Lateran Pact, Mussolini's attitude provoked some tension in relations with the Holy See. In the summer of 1930, this tension was felt again, but much more intensely, because the government refused to allow Catholic Action to continue with its activities in trade unionism and sport. In the end Pius XI gave way, persuaded by, among others, Cardinals Gasparri and Pacelli, because he

* The lay arm of the Church, founded in 1865, when the papacy lost its temporal power. [Translator's note.]

felt it was not the time to quarrel with fascism, when the real enemy was, increasingly, communism.

Apart from these moments of strain, relations between fascist Italy and the Holy See were on the whole correct, even if not always cordial, until 1938.

4

QUOTA 90

A FUNDAMENTAL problem of the European economy after the war was that of curbing the inflation which, to a greater or lesser extent, had struck all its currencies; these had to be revalued and stabilized. This deflationary policy made difficulties for the development which was taking place during the twenties, encouraged the merging of firms, and was paid for by the workers, who suffered a high rate of unemployment. Particularly important was the exchange rate of the pound, still considered the leading currency in the world economy (although by then it was sharing this position with the dollar). Once the post-war crisis was over, Britain pursued a strongly deflationary policy under Churchill, then Chancellor of the Exchequer. In 1925 the pound went back to its pre-war value in relation to the dollar and returned also to free convertibility into gold. It was basically a policy of imperial prestige which, although justified by the wish not to lose its leading position in the world money market, no longer had an adequate basis in reality (the war had meant that vast quantities of gold had been transferred from Europe and Britain to America), and put a very strong brake on the country's industrial development.

In August 1926, in a speech at Pesaro, Mussolini announced a drastic policy of deflation. The lira's value had been declining ever since the war, and by 1926 its value was about a seventh of what it had been before the war. It now had to be revalued in such a way that about 90 lire corresponded to the value of £1 sterling: *quota novanta*, as it was called, in fighting terms. The quota was reached in December 1927;

the official value of the lira went up to a quarter, then to a third, of what it had been before the war.

This operation was carried out by the Minister of Finance, who was then Count Giuseppe Volpi, one of the most important financiers in Italy. Volpi had succeeded De Stefani in 1925 because De Stefani had upset the business world. Since Volpi was trusted by the business world, he was particularly suited to undertake an operation which led to a good deal of perplexity and aroused much opposition. Besides, in choosing a minister of Finance (the key minister in the economic policy of the country, in spite of the much publicized Minister of the Corporations) Mussolini always followed this rule: to give preference to a technical expert or to a civil servant when it was a matter of implementing classical economic policy, that is, of limited public interference in the economy (De Stefani had been one such minister, and Mosconi, minister from 1928–32, was to be another); but to give preference to someone directly connected with the financial world when it was a matter of pursuing a policy of public intervention, which might favour the business world but might also arouse its suspicion and hostility (Volpi was one such minister, and so were Jung and, to some extent, Thaon de Revel, ministers from 1932–40).

There were various reasons for the revaluation of the lira. Some were reasons of prestige: particularly around 3 January 1925, the foreign stock exchanges (London's, for instance) had made attempts to speculate on the fall of the lira, taking advantage of the economic as well as the political circumstances at the time; then, too, in its official statements fascism was beginning to rant furiously against what it called the international plutocracy of Jews and freemasons. Another reason lay in the effort made to lighten the burden of imports; another in the effort to improve the financial and industrial establishment by drastically deflating the more inflationary parts of it. Also, an attempt was made to favour those who held government stock, and foreign capital invested in Italy, at a time when the rhythm of private investments was slowing down, but could be compensated for by an increase in public and foreign investments.

The revaluation of the lira had important consequences for Italy's economy. It favoured the electrical firms, which brought in capital, and, in general, the importers of raw materials; it damaged the other industries, banks involved in financing industry, the industrial export trade and dealers in farm produce. Businessmen had strong reservations about it. The majority of them favoured the revaluation and in particular the stabilization of the lira, but they thought the rate Mussolini had imposed was too high. Textile manufacturers were particularly angry about it, being more involved in exporting than any others. The financier Gualino, who controlled the artificial silk industry, and who the previous year had greatly increased the capital of Snia Viscosa, wrote a furiously indignant letter to Mussolini.

But other results of the policy of deflation were more important; the fact that, as Vittorio Foa had pointed out, it broadened the basis of fascism by bringing together parts of the lower middle class on fixed incomes and the upper middle class, and dealt a blow to the working-class movement and its industrial claims; it was also a determining factor in stopping the rise of new firms, favouring mergers between those already in existence, and stabilizing the status quo in the economic and social world. (The process of concentration and merging greatly helped mining, electrical, chemical and ship-building firms.) A similar result was achieved by the return to protectionism, brought in by Volpi as early as 1925.

When Mussolini launched his directive on quota 90, he did

not mean to favour the large firms so much as to strengthen the state financially at the expense of the private sector. Of course he had no wish to curb the development of the big firms, which were the pillar of the national economy. But he did dislike, and suspected, large economic concentrations of power, both financial (like the Banca Commerciale) and industrial (like Fiat), and would have liked to control their development. He disliked, and suspected, the supposed international connections of the Banca Commerciale and its tendency to depend upon inflation; and the high profits of the Fiat monopoly and its way of imposing its wishes, against those of the state (for instance, in matters of customs duties). However, this was certainly not the only time in which Mussolini's economic policy had results which, to a limited but in some ways quite significant extent, were diametrically opposed to what he would really have liked to see.

In order to understand the persistent foolishness of Mussolini's 'anti-monopolistic' intentions one must bear in mind the fact that he meant economic production to serve solely as an instrument of national power. An economic policy in which the problem of the redistribution of wealth and individual prosperity were entirely secondary automatically favoured the large producers at the expense of those of middle size. The objective consequences of the Pesaro policy, some of which were not deliberately sought, actually conflicted with some of Mussolini's foolish ideas, but, as I have already said, they helped to renew and even more to strengthen the traditional checks and balances in society and to make the state more fascist.

At this point it seems suitable to attempt a general judgement (anticipating what will be said later), and to say that fascism, considered as a whole, was the political régime of large-scale Italian capital in a time of crisis (the whole inter-war period was a time of crisis). Insofar as it was such a régime, fascism amplified and almost institutionalized the fundamental characteristics of capital, that is, the promoting of a limited development while, at the same time, deepening imbalances (and not only those between north and south) and consolidating monopolistic tendencies that checked development itself. But the relationship between fascism and large-scale capital was not simple and straightforward (as it appeared to the French scholar Guérin), but complex, twisted and even contradictory. Examples which illustrate this contorted relationship are the demands of the left-wing fascists and the trade unionists, the half-hearted anti-monopolistic tendencies, the need to reinforce the public sector in relation to the private sector, the requirements of public works and after 1936 the attempt at a policy of economic planning. But it is no coincidence that each ended in failure, though in different degrees.

The policy introduced in the Pesaro speech had its effect only in 1927 on the expansion of the most important industries (mining, electrical, metallurgical, chemical, building, textile). It lessened the importance of the less concentrated part of industry – the textile industry – and increased the importance of the more concentrated sectors, in the first place the electrical industry, which for several years had held a dominant position in the Italian industrial system.

By the end of 1927 and with the stabilizing of the lira at quota 90, the big industries had in fact overcome their difficulties. In 1928 and 1929 the crisis was felt mainly by the medium-sized and small industries (which sought to save themselves with a large number of mergers) as well as in agriculture.

Statistics appear to show an increase in *per capita* income during those years. Nevertheless, Italy remained one of the poorest countries. It has been calculated that the average income of an employed Italian in the period 1924–34 was less than a quarter of an American's, less than a third of an Englishman's, less than half of a Frenchman's. Among the main nations of the world, apart from the USSR and Yugoslavia, Italy was the poorest.

De Stefani had increased taxes. Volpi, who remained in office until 1928, noticeably reduced them. Above all, taxes which weighed on the property-owning classes were lowered: taxes on movable property, registration taxes and estate duty, taxes on trade. But the reduction of taxes on trade, combined with deflation, had beneficial effects on the rise in the cost of living. Official figures indicate that real wages, both industrial and agricultural, were rising: nominally, wages went down, but the cost of living went down even faster. Food improved, at least for some of the population: the number of calories per head was greater than it had been in the years 1923–5.

But the policy announced at Pesaro meant an enormous increase in unemployment. This was particularly so in the country, which was suffering from a double set of misfortunes: on the one hand internal inflation and on the other, from 1927 onwards, the fall in international prices, which was particularly sharp in agriculture. The crisis provoked by the Pesaro policy struck particularly at the many small farmers – tenants and *mezzadri* who had borrowed money with which to buy land. Both crises hit the south in particular, for there the expensive crops were intended for export. The drop in exports helped to exacerbate the Southern Question. In the period between the two world wars agricultural production increased by 22 per cent in the north, and by 3 per cent in the south; that is, in the south it diminished, if one omits corn production.

In 1928 the government tried to relieve agricultural difficulties and unemployment by two means, first, it increased corn production (this was known as 'the battle for wheat');

secondly, it introduced a large programme of public works.

The battle for wheat had already been started, in fact, by Volpi in July 1925, when he restored the protective tax on wheat. This tax was later increased, in September 1928, and then again in June 1930, at the beginning of the Depression. Later it was reduced.

The objectives of the battle for wheat were to improve the country's economic balance (wheat had one of the biggest import duties on it), to protect national wheat production from monetary deflation and the lowering of international prices, and to increase production and reach self-sufficiency in a fundamental sector of the nation's food. Good efforts were made to improve production as a whole, and almost enough wheat was produced to supply the nation's needs. The efforts made to improve production were correct. Production rose almost enough to cover national needs. The use of artificial fertilizers increased enormously; compared with 1922, it had almost doubled in 1926, and more than doubled in 1929, then, during the Depression, it greatly decreased. This favoured agricultural practice to a remarkable degree, and the expansion of the firm of Montecatini, which, with its tight monopoly, imposed high prices on fertilizers, and thus made the agricultural crisis worse.

On the other hand, the favours granted to wheat producers were given to the large farmers, and this struck again at the small man. Animal husbandry, a fundamental part of modern agriculture, was also damaged. Besides, the measures taken for protective reasons in Italy kept prices there higher than they were on the international market, diminishing the effects of deflation on the cost of living, with further harm to the less prosperous.

Public works centred on land reclamation : what was called 'integral drainage', under the leadership of an eminent agronomist, Arrigo Serpieri. Volpo, who had used public money to bolster up industry, was replaced as Minister of Finance by Antonio Mosconi, who was told to favour public works quite definitely. In order to finance them, Mosconi increased taxation, which from then onwards, in spite of efforts made until 1930 to bring it down, continued to rise uninterruptedly. From 1929 onwards Italy had the highest rate of taxation of any of the major nations. The increase in taxes as a whole, however, was made mainly through indirect taxation.

Work on land drainage and reclamation took place mostly between 1928 and 1933. Its aim was not so much to change social relations linked to the exploitation and ownership of land as to improve production technically. In many cases it favoured speculation in land by large firms which came into being purely in the hope of profit. Fascism, which spent almost as much as governments had spent on such works between 1870 and 1922, considered its land drainage programme (the Pontine Marshes, for instance) with special satisfaction for, among other things, its spectacular propaganda value. And indeed, in spite of its high price (which, on the other hand, showed the intensity of the effort), the land drainage programme was a success for the régime. In this field fascism executed some parts of the programme of the democratic Italian left for example, that associated with Garibaldi's name). The reform of the Sicilian *latifondi*, decided upon shortly before the outbreak of the Second World War, never got beyond the planning stage, however.

In spite of these public works, the conditions of the working class grew worse in 1929. The use of basic consumer goods began to diminish. As the peasants poured into the towns in search of work and there was little work to be found there, the government took measures to prevent this tendency to settle in towns, and then widened these powers, which had first come into operation in March 1926.

Linked with what has been called the ruralism of the fascist régime in general, and of Mussolini in particular, was the policy of population growth. This was an aspect of ruralism (an altogether larger phenomenon) which had the same objectives as Mussolini's foreign policy. The growth in population (which, in any case, was very small) was desired above all because it was thought that numbers meant power and because this increase was the best method of propaganda with which to justify fascism's expansionist aspirations to Italian public opinion and to foreign governments (in particular the British).

Judged by today's standards, the policy of population growth now seems all the more irrational from the economic point of view, since it was also meant to be the reply to America – first North, then South America – which was closing its doors to Italian immigration. Mussolini, exceedingly touched about anything to do with national prestige and dignity, in his turn placed prohibitions and limitations on emigration between 1925 and 1927.

Ruralism meant that the country was exalted as something stable and conservative, a storehouse to prevent too many people going into the towns, where the unemployed were more visible (thus damaging the régime's prestige) and the working classes could more easily disrupt public order. Fascist propaganda idealized the country in a sickly, false kind of way. Its real object was to control social mobility very strictly at the roots. This gave the rich a pleasant sense of security. In the final years of the régime a harmless little song was sung, the words of which ran: 'O woodman, the sun is setting, leave your work, and come home to your hut.' That the woodman's life consisted of work until sunset, that he lived in a hut, and that there was no possibility of change, were perfectly obvious facts, accepted as natural because they had always existed and had become customary. This does not mean, of course, that during the twenty years of fascism workmen ceased to pour into the towns, attracted by industrial development (after 1935, industry became more important than agriculture in terms of national production); it means merely that the flow was carefully controlled.

What was called the rural policy was also the means by which Mussolini tried to hide their deteriorating conditions from the peasants. Fascist propaganda gave the peasant's small-holding an exalted, mythical air at exactly the time when, in real life, the policy of *quota* 90 and the tax on wheat were dragging it down. Admittedly one of the aims of the land drainage programme was to develop the small-holdings. But, compared with the basic developments in the countryside, it had little success. This really meant that, as Mussolini's foolish wish to control the large firms ended up by giving them more power, so the propaganda praising the small-holder was really hiding the increasing power of the big landowner.

However much or however little people in 1925-9 were aware of it, protectionism, the revaluation of the lira, the battle for wheat, and the measures taken against people flooding into the towns all appear to the historian seeking to see them rationally as parts of a general effort to curb the mobility of the economy and of society, to stabilize the situation and to place it under the strict control of the richer classes. There were many dark corners in the picture. Social stability was paid for by a frustrated, unbalanced economic development: frustrated by the crisis which *quota* 90 provoked in the country, unbalanced because the general troubles in the country limited developments to the big firms. All the same (and this applies to the previous chapter as well), the ruling classes felt that there was much more light than darkness about it all.

Perhaps the real nature of the sympathies of the ruling

classes, and of the way in which the régime, with its orderliness and the lack of social mobility, which contrasted so strongly with the unforgotten 'two red years', answered their profound aspirations, can be found in the links between fascism itself and an important part (not only the most superficial, noisy or opportunist part of it, either) of the ethical and political culture of the years preceding it.

Over-simplifying, perhaps, one may say that fascism was the most sensational result, and the conclusion, of that culture, which had been, above all, spiritual, anti-materialist, anti-positivist and anti-democratic. Benedetto Croce, who had been its main representative, gave fascism a number of its cultural starting-points; we should not, however, forget the profoundly and steadily liberal character of a philosophy which, like Croce's, was entirely based on the distinction between the various moments of the spirit.

The other great Italian philosopher, Giovanni Gentile, was rather different. He carried forward, in a speculative way, the philosophical revaluation initiated by Croce, emphasizing the unity of the spirit and its dynamic, aggressive character. A richly human man, he felt a profound need for religion and a generous urge to test culture in the crucible of everyday life, and of politics. This generosity was mixed, rather touchingly, with a complete lack of good sense. It might be said that Gentile felt reality should base itself on his consistent metaphysical speculations, and not vice versa. He passed from liberalism to fascism – and was faithful to it until death – because he thought he could see put into practice in its brutality the moral lesson of Francesco De Sanctis, that is, an ethical and religious reform of the traditional sceptical, smiling Italian character.

But Gentile himself, with his formalism (which can also be found in the important educational reform he carried through) helped, without meaning to, to give a kind of status to the moral and cultural insanity of fascism. Fascism – he said – was not a system but thought in the making; it was culture because culture is form and style, not substance and content. Plenty of damaged goods were hidden under that form or style. One of the fundamental defects of fascism, as I have said, was the gap that often yawned between its statements and doctrines and its concrete attitudes and actions.

The similar way in which an eminent historian, Gioacchino Volpe, moved from liberalism to fascism is also remarkably interesting. As a first-rate historian, he was no formalist. But in his fascism, there was something of Gentile's blind generosity : perhaps because of his love of life, which meant he was able to evoke it in the past in so masterly a way. He turned to fascism in November 1920, just when it was beginning to have its first successes as a reaction to socialism. But very soon he wished it to go beyond this purely negative stage. In fascism he saw the possibility of a higher degree of moral tension, of a more powerful foreign policy and of a wider participation, by the masses, in the bourgeois state. As long as he was able to do so, he tried to save the small amount of freedom compatible with the system. Then his voice grew steadily weaker. But he said, as if casually, that the dictatorship of the fascist régime was quite incidental.

In this general cultural climate Alfredo Rocco, an eminent Nationalist jurist and the Minister of Justice, was able, between 1925 and 1929, to build up the juridical structure of the new state : a state that was strictly reactionary and totalitarian in its intentions, an abstractly perfect machine which would concentrate all power in the hands of a more or less imaginary ruling class, a kind of patrician stratum of the best minds. Although this rigour might seem interestingly indicative of certain authoritarian tendencies present today in the background of neo-capitalist economy and society, the state which was Rocco's idea and which he created already had serious faults and limitations in 1929.

These faults and limitations were of two kinds. In the first place, the reactionary nature of this state meant that nothing in it acted as a balance to the ruling class. In the second place, the totalitarianism was itself limited through the existence of centres of power outside the state, such as the Church and the monarchy. A further limitation, less serious but more intrinsic, was connected with the relationship between the state and economic policy. Whatever Rocco himself felt about quota 90, it certainly helped the establishment of a totalitarian state to a remarkable degree. Nevertheless, its limitations lay in the very compromise, established, in point of fact, between the authoritarian coherence of the juridical order, which, on the level of economic policy, implied the preeminence of public spending and of the industries linked with it, and the opposite tendency which aimed to contain public spending within the industrial sector and to keep down the pressure of taxation. But, when all this has been said, it must be added at once that quota 90 strengthened the possibility of public intervention in a number of ways, that from 1928 onwards taxes and public expenditure continued to rise, and that the programme of public works on the 'imperial' replanning of Rome was enlarged in 1931 at Rocco's suggestion, and warmly welcomed by Mussolini.

In 1929 the state was coherent in form but fundamentally unstable. Although it sought to be as firm and immovable as granite, its own lack of any real internal balance forced it to evolve very quickly. Two opposing kinds of evolution appeared in it: one put forward by the moderate fascists, such as Grandi and Volpe, who even wished for a partial, controlled restoration of freedom, while keeping the reactionary structure built up over the past few years as the leading elements of the whole system; the other wishing to extend totalitarianism, somehow making the mass of the people participants in it, and passing from the nationalist state created by Rocco to the fully fascist state.

This second type of evolution prevailed. The world economic crisis of the thirties certainly played an important part in encouraging it, but it must be added that this second type had always been the kind most congenial to Mussolini's own temperament and aspirations. But in a society like that of Italy, a society that was not at all homogeneous and had several centres of power, totalitarianism could be achieved only with powerful inconsistencies – 'Italian-style', in other words. Rocco's consistency involuntarily paved the way for the era of Starace.

5

FOREIGN POLICY

FROM the beginning Mussolini took a particular interest in foreign policy. It was said that fascism subordinated internal policy to foreign policy. The opposite was also true: in his foreign policy Mussolini sought for successes and diversions to emphasize or consolidate the prestige of fascism at home. But on the whole the first remark held the greater truth.

In its early days, fascism had claimed to be against all imperialism, Italy's own, and that of other states. But very soon this was altered radically, not just because nationalistic ideologies and interests prevailed but also because Britain and France were showing imperialistic tendencies. In arguing with those who were called the *renunciatori*,* fascism meant to put up an energetic opposition to British and French imperialism.

With a few exceptions, Mussolini's relations with foreign policy were like an unhappy love affair. He was a party leader rather than a statesman; a master in the art of undermining the structure of the state, but less skilful at building it up and, in particular, at consolidating it. He seemed to realize, in a muddled sort of way, that all was not well when he had to act outside Italy and away from his audience. He did not feel at ease in dealing on equal terms with people who, though formally they might behave correctly, were opposed to him. Between 1922 and 1925 he went abroad three times: to Lausanne, to London and then, reluctantly, to Locarno. After that, he never went out of Italy again until his meet-

*See page 12

ings with Hitler. The bold timidity with which he react
when he found himself among hostile, anti-fascist people
the foreign correspondents whom he had met at Locarno,
instance – was indicative of his general attitude.

Considering the twenty years of fascism as a whole, it c
be said that foreign policy was the régime's weak poin
whereas between 1922 and 1929 there were remarkable s
cesses, in a conservative sense, at home. For a number
reasons these successes turned out to be short-lived. I me
tioned some of them in the previous chapter. But the decisi
reasons for the collapse of fascism can be found in its forei
policy. Its extremist, subversive tendencies, kept under co
trol at home in order not to antagonize the conservatives,
foreign policy remained active and finally became dominan

In a few words it is, of course, hard to sum fascism up
a balanced way : it is hard to estimate the damage it caus
in terms of moral, civil and political values. If, however, o
had to sum up what fascism meant in the history of Ita
one might say that it allowed the conservative ruling class
to put off, for between twenty and twenty-five years, t
social problems which, born in the years 1919–22 and stifl
by fascism, were brought up again after 25 July 1943 a
25 April 1945; and that this advantage gained by the co
servatives was paid for by the country because it involved
in a disastrous war.

However, we should not consider the foreign policy
fascism as something complete in itself, or fail to consider
various internal phases. The foreign policy followed un
1932 and, in some ways, until 1935 was profoundly differe
from that which followed after 1935. During the early peri
a peaceable line was taken, on the whole, which allow
Italy to exploit fascism's diplomatic trump card at lea
as far as the Foreign Ministry, and later Grandi, whe
he was in charge of it between 1929 and 1932, were co

ned. This trump card was the fact that conservatives all
er the world considered fascist Italy a bulwark against
shevism in Europe, and accorded it a respect they had not
orded to Italy when it was liberal. French newspapers of
period show this change of attitude very clearly : before
2 they were scornful of Italy, as a place of social instability;
er 1922, full of interest and respect for it, as a country
ich, thanks to fascism, had achieved public order.

n the early years of fascism, as I have said, its foreign
icy was a peaceable one. Today it is considered that it was
eaceable policy in substance, interrupted occasionally by
like speeches from Mussolini, which were bombastic but
mless. However, this idea can, with greater truth, be
ied upside down : until 1932–5 fascism's foreign policy
generally more peaceable in form than in substance.
art from his aggressive speeches, Mussolini pursued a
ceable foreign policy because he felt that there was no
sibility of war in Europe for the time being. But the possi-
ty of war was always in the back of his mind and, while
ting for it, he was constantly anxious to keep the in-
national situation fluid; admittedly favouring peaceful
tions between the states, but at the same time trying to
vent these relations from settling down and becoming
solidated. For Mussolini, peace was never an end in itself;
most it was a means. What in diplomatic language is
own as the permanent interest of a state did not, in the
e of fascist Italy, coincide with peace. This fundamental
t meant that fascist Italy, although it loved to exalt itself
a great power, really denied itself the prerogatives of a
eat, victorious nation (which, among other things, is re-
onsible with other nations for the international order) and
haved like some small, restless Balkan state.

In international relations, Mussolini tried to follow,
utatis mutandis, a policy similar to that which he had

pursued so successfully at home in his relations with other parties and other power groups: a policy that alternated with dizzying speed between, or else actually used at the same time, gentleness and arrogance; at one point trying to reach agreement, immediately afterwards sticking out obstinately for what he wanted. In international relations he behaved throughout all, or nearly all, his years in power in the restless, changeable, dynamic way which was characteristic of him as a diplomatist and, indeed, as a man. The international political situation favoured him to a remarkable degree. In the inter-war years it was dominated by three fundamental elements: France's fear of Germany; the conservative classes' fear of communism; and the conflict of the defeated countries and the victorious countries over the revision of the peace treaties. Mussolini exploited all three elements.

Up to 1932 his foreign policy went through several phases: a first phase from 1922 to 1925, a second from 1925 to December 1927, and a third from January 1928 to 1932.

During the first phase, which was by far the best, he took the diplomatic line laid down by Salvatore Contarini, Secretary-General of the Foreign Ministry. He followed a traditional, moderate foreign policy (the Corfu episode, however important, was an exception), either to reassure foreign governments, or because in 1924 he was taken up with home affairs, or else because, for some months, illness made him neglect public affairs. Contarini, whose support of nationalism fused with the foreign policy initiated by Count Sforza, intended to continue along the same lines, while at the same time emphasizing elements that would serve to promote rivalry with, and bring pressure to bear upon, France, and on its policy of keeping the *status quo*. It was European diplomacy on a broad scale with particular emphasis on the Danube and Balkan area; intended to make Italy instead of France the central figure and guide for all the states in that area, starting with Yugoslavia, and, at the same time, to consolidate the international order in Europe, making the most of friendship with Britain, weakening French leadership on the continent and bringing Bolshevik Russia in again as a balancing factor.

Italy's policy towards Yugoslavia, which led to the signing of a treaty of friendship in January 1924, had precedents in some of Mussolini's own attitudes. Long before the March on Rome he had criticized what might be called the Adriatic obsession of Sonnino's diplomacy and of the so-called Dalmatophils. This obsession, which was cunningly encouraged by the Allies, had meant that Italian diplomacy was concentrated upon Dalmatia; this had helped keep it out of the Mediterranean and the share-out of colonial spoils. The fact was that Mussolini's attitude towards Yugoslavia was one of bitter, contemptuous hostility, born of nationalism and of D'Annunzian ideas, yet alternating with occasional phases in which there was an easing of tension. Paradoxically, he longed to obtain both the advantages of a policy that would strangle and destroy the state of Yugoslavia, and those of a policy of friendship and peaceful economic penetration – a policy much desired by, among others, the Italian industrialists. Essentially, Mussolini was always ready to get on well with Yugoslavia, but after 1925 he nearly always laid down conditions which the government in Belgrade could not agree to without prejudice to its own national security.

What was called the Contarini period of fascist foreign policy had its triumph in October 1925 when Italy signed the Locarno Pact; this diminished France's continental leadership, based on the *status quo* and the League of Nations, and favoured a more flexible diplomacy under the guidance of the four western powers.

But in 1925 a new phase began in fascist foreign policy, a phase that became progressively less moderate and was characterized by pronounced verbal aggressiveness, directed sometimes against Turkey, sometimes against Ethiopia, sometimes against Yugoslavia and sometimes against France. The cordial relations with Britain, which were the lynch-pin of fascist foreign policy from 1924–35, contrasted with this aggressiveness. On the other hand, conservative Britain found that, if he was kept severely in check, Mussolini was useful for two reasons: first, in order to balance the power of France on the continent, particularly in the Danube and Balkan area, and in the Mediterranean; and secondly, to guarantee the social order against any possible communist movements. Several times, both publicly and privately, Churchill and the Foreign Secretary Austen Chamberlain praised Mussolini in pro-fascist, anti-communist statements. Friendship with Britain in the second half of 1924 gave Mussolini a support that helped him to overcome the crisis following the murder of Matteotti.

Gradually, between early 1925 and early 1926, Contarini was more and more neglected and finally removed; this was due, among other things, to the pressure of fascist extremists under the leadership of Giunta and Farinacci. The diplomatic star of Dino Grandi then began to rise. Foreign policy, like other branches of the state, was to be 'made fascist'. The 'fierce face' which Mussolini showed the outside world was meant to spread fear and raise the value of agreement with him; it was also probably trying to hide the difficulties inherent in the revaluation of the lira and of its prestige on foreign markets. Mussolini stopped showing his 'fierce face' in December 1927. The decisive reason for this was a warning from Britain, which threatened to abandon him for standing up too strongly in France; Britain, indeed, later became friendlier with France. But the change coincided – fortuitously, perhaps – with the stabilizing of the lira.

Relations with France between 1925 and 1927 went

through periods of very great tension. There were reasons for conflict, both in the Mediterranean (Tunis and Tangiers) and in the Danube and Balkan area, and Contarini had used them as a means of keeping moderate but constant pressure on France. Mussolini pushed Contarini's policy to the limit and added another element to it, one that to him was of fundamental importance: the ideological element which placed fascism in opposition to democracy and anti-fascism. He was annoyed with France in particular because of the support which Italian exiles, and anti-fascism in general, found there. In April 1926, during a visit to Libya, he exalted – alluding to France and also Turkey – the *mare nostrum*, and for the first time clearly set fascism up against the democratic world. Although fascism was not yet a commodity for export, the possibility of it spreading in Europe was already apparent. A number of examples encouraged Mussolini: Primo de Rivera's régime in Spain, for instance, already established for several years; while Poland, Portugal and Lithuania were all adopting authoritarian and in varying degrees illiberal régimes at about that time.

As I have said, the decisive factor which made Mussolini moderate his dynamic foreign policy at the end of 1927 was a warning from Britain, which became friendly with France and left Italy isolated. This was the concrete and decisive reason for his altered behaviour, but there were other more general causes which should be borne in mind, quite apart from the revaluation of the lira, mentioned earlier. Collaboration between France and Germany was becoming increasingly difficult and Mussolini saw before him a broad field for diplomatic manoeuvre, using Germany to put pressure upon France. The Italian state had now been thoroughly 'made fascist' and abroad the régime was held in very high esteem. This meant that aggressive attitudes had become unnecessary, indeed counter-productive, particularly since the rest of the world seemed to be veering towards peace. The policy of public works and land drainage, too, meant that it was best to curb military expenditure and in international relations to pursue the principle of disarmament.

Relations with France, which were a thermometer of Mussolini's diplomacy, improved. In April 1924 (when the left-wing alliance was in the ascendant) Poincaré had refused to consider Mussolini's request that he should take measures against Italian political exiles in France. Now, at the end of 1927, Poincaré took these measures, having meantime returned to power after the intervening period of left-wing governments. Other similar measures were taken the following year. At the same time, between April and July 1928, Italy obtained satisfaction over the question of Tangiers.* In 1928, a policy of cordial relations with Ethiopia was pursued, which led, in August of the same year, to a treaty of friendship.

On 5 June 1928, Mussolini made statements of a definitely peaceable kind, while keeping up a programme of moderate revisionism as far as the treaties were concerned. The most sensitive area was that of the Danube and the Balkans: hostility against the Little Entente, particularly against Yugoslavia, and support for Hungarian and Bulgarian revisionism, were quite open. Mussolini also repeated a statement which he had made in May of the previous year: between 1935 and 1940, he said, Europe would go through a crucially important period. Like many other politicians he felt that the end of the occupation of the Rhineland, planned for 1935, would bring the problem of Germany's international position and of the revision of the Treaty of Versailles into sharp relief. There was no threatening tone in this statement, however;

* In 1923, Italy had been excluded from the international arrangements made for Tangiers, in which Britain, France and Spain were involved.

rather it appeared to be inviting the powers to avoid the danger of more serious complications by a timely, reasonable revision of the treaties.

Under this peaceable façade, however, there lurked a more complex reality. Mussolini never abandoned his object of keeping the international situation fluid, and, at some future date, of secretly helping the many irredentist movements created by the peace treaties.

The need to revise these treaties had already been stated publicly by him as early as January 1922. This need expressed, first of all, the post-war troubles in Italy. But a reasonable, moderate revision of the treaties, which would eliminate, or at least improve, their worst aspects, was considered sympathetically by public opinion in large areas of Europe, particularly in socialist and democratic circles. There were two possible sorts of revisionism: one which was peaceful in the methods it used and moderate in its objectives; the other, violent in its methods and radical in its objectives. The first was supported by the socialists and democrats, the second by the nationalists of the vanquished nations. Mussolini showed both attitudes alternately, the peaceable and the violent, and this disconcerting way of changing his attitude made it hard, even before 1935, to believe that he had any really peaceful intentions.

An intermittent but lively secret revisionism had already appeared in 1923, at the time of the incident in Corfu. Secretly, Mussolini had been in touch with the Macedonian nationalists and with the extreme right in Germany; while Stresemann, the German Foreign Minister, had rejected such advances, made with a view to a future conflict with Yugoslavia. Later, in 1925, Mussolini was secretly in touch with the Moroccan rebel Abd el-Krim; later still, in 1927, there was the treaty with Hungary.

In other words, Mussolini's revisionism was aimed, in a

confused way, in several different directions: at Europe in the Danube and Balkan area, at Germany, and also at Morocco. Morocco showed his wish for a new arrangement of the Western Mediterranean, which would work against France; and, in the distance, it was possible to see a plan to exploit the Arab movement against colonial domination. At the same time, on another point – that of the Cyrenaican-Egyptian border, which implied a state of rebellion in Cyrenaica – Mussolini declared that he agreed unreservedly with Austen Chamberlain on the need for the European powers to present a united front on questions relating to the Arab world and to the East.

The fascist government's irredentist tendencies were, however, strongly curbed in Austria because of the problem of the *Anschluss* (the union of Austria and Germany) and that of Tyrolean irredentism in the Alto Adige. On these matters it was wholly in Italy's interests strictly to support the conditions laid down by the peace treaties. But about 1928 Italy began to be much less severe in its attitude, chiefly because Austria and Italy began to draw closer together, and later fascist Italy began to take over the leadership in Austria from Stresemann's Germany. The reasons for this were the weakness of the Austrian socialists and the strength of the right-wing parties, the main result of which was the discouragement given to the irredentist movement in the Tyrol by the government in Vienna.

Thus, while he was initiating a phase of more unambiguously peaceable policy in relation to the other great powers, Mussolini was able to consider clearly his own revisionist policy. This had its field of action in the Danube and Balkan area of Europe, its main adversary in Yugoslavia, its strong points in Hungary and Albania, and its tools in the irredentist movements of the various national minorities; in the first place, the Croats. Yugoslavia was, together with Ethiopia, one of the main zones of fascist expansion. Behind Yugo-slavia loomed the whole Danube and Balkan area, where Mussolini and his colleagues hoped more than once to form a political or economic group of states under the leadership of Italy. Since these hopes were always rebuffed, mainly because of their all-too-obvious anti-French and revisionistic character, fascism's policy in the area consisted of a tenacious but vain series of diplomatic initiatives aimed at the individual states there. The result, unlike the result in Ethiopia, was unsuccessful. Fascist activity there served only as a foretaste of what, with a very different degree of strength, Nazi Germany was later to do.

It would be a mistake, however, to overemphasize these aspects of fascist foreign policy and to neglect its authentically peaceable side. In 1929, on the very eve of the Depression, various changes made among ministers confirmed the peaceable direction of foreign policy and, in home affairs, the effort gradually to consolidate, in a conservative way, the institutions set up by Rocco. Mussolini gave up the direction of the Foreign Ministry and handed it over to Grandi, who had been Under-Secretary there since 1925. He also gave up the direction of other ministries which until then had been in his hands, and passed them over to colleagues. One of the most important appointments was that of Bottai as Minister of the Corporations, at which he had, until then, been Under-Secretary; and another, because of this ministry's special importance, was the appointment of another moderate, Leandro Arpinati, as Under-Secretary of the Interior.

The wish to carry out a peaceable foreign policy was further confirmed, in the early days of the Depression, when Grandi was able to develop it to a degree which had not been seen since 1925. For a number of reasons Mussolini allowed Grandi his experiment. In 1929–30 the Concordat seemed to bring the fascist state and the Catholic Church close together on a common conservative platform. Intransigent attitudes were discouraged among the fascists; in the Catholic Church, the trend towards union with eastern churches and towards a loosening of links with the imperialism of the western powers was also discouraged, and an ever more rigid anti-communism prevailed. Relations between the fascist state and the Catholic Church, having passed the crisis of 1931, reached the height of cordiality during the Ethiopian war. The attitude of Pius XI in these circumstances, substantially supporting the enterprise, was in clear contrast to the cautious attitude maintained by the Pope towards imperialism in the twenties.

On the other hand, the Depression, although it made the working-class movement more radical everywhere, in some countries (Britain for instance) encouraged the tendency towards class collaboration. In this, there was now room for Mussolini to manoeuvre, for fascism was seen as a variant of this same collaboration, and one that would be less damaging to the entrepreneur. (The communist idea, which was popular at the time, of the equal status of social democracy and fascism appears to be confirmed here.)

Grandi went further than Mussolini in his plans: he meant to exploit the situation as far as he possibly could and to use fascism in its moderate version as a wedge to divide the newly-born front of international anti-fascism. In this he was helped by the revisionist sympathies and the very definite pacifism of the labour politicians in power in Britain, and particularly by his personal friendship with the Foreign Minister, the socialist Henderson. It is possible, in fact, that one of the reasons why Mussolini allowed Grandi to take over foreign affairs was that he could thus exploit the revisionism supported by the labour politicians, and the dislike of France's continental leadership and its reluctance to disarm, which was widespread both among the Labour Party supporters and American public opinion.

Apart from this general reason, Mussolini had two other more immediate motives, deriving from issues which dominated the international scene in those years, for taking a peaceable tone in foreign affairs: one was the reduction of Germany's war reparations and the other – a decisive one – was disarmament. On both these Italy's interests were the same as those of its ex-wartime allies, Britain and France, although very careful negotiations were required. The solution of both problems, the second one in particular, was universally felt to be a prerequisite for ending the Depression, because it would help to curb military spending and, people said, would promote peace and world trade. Mussolini wanted disarmament in order to finish his public works, and because it was the least costly way of keeping up threats and pressure on France, in a more or less distant future.

Grandi's policy was one of friendship with Britain and a new approach to France. In line with the two general aims was his effort to emphasize the peaceful nature of Italy's penetration into the Balkans, and to come to an agreement with Yugoslavia. He also tried to emphasize the moderate nature of Italy's penetration along the Danube, favouring the Habsburg restoration, and the fact that it was merely defensive against Germany. Very cautiously, too, he pressed Italian expansionist claims against Ethiopia, conceived as a classic case of colonial activity which could be undertaken in close agreement with the other interested powers, Britain and France. From 1929 onwards a policy of pressure from Somalia to the Ethiopian Ogaden was pursued; the incident of WalWal, in 1934, was a later result of this policy.

Grandi's experiment, however, could already be considered to have failed substantially by the early part of 1931, and it was the object of growing criticism from extreme fascists – Italo Balbo, in the first place. Grandi's activity followed a course similar to that of the possible 'positive' developments of fascism in home affairs. 1930 was the year of illusion and hope, 1931 the year of disillusion and disappointment, during which a decisive turn was taken in home affairs and economic policy. 1932 was the year in which Mussolini drew his conclusions from the disappointments of the previous year. It is significant that, as far as one can see, in 1931 he returned to the close personal direction of foreign policy. Only once, in May 1930, did he apply his habitual 'fierce face' tactic towards France, in order to persuade it to agree on disarmament. Grandi and his colleagues disapproved of the 'fierce face' tactic, and of the excesses of the fascist press, because they hardened attitudes in France into anti-fascist and anti-Italian prejudice. 1931 was also the year of conflict with the Church; the year in which Grandi took up again, on a bigger scale, his anti-Yugoslav intrigues with Ante Pavelic's Croation movement; the year in which, as the Depression worsened, hopes held in 1930 that an economic sector dominated by Italy could be established in the Danube and Balkan area were dashed.

The decisive factor which made Mussolini dismiss Grandi in July 1932 was the double defeat suffered over the problem first of reparations and then of disarmament, in which Italy was left high and dry by Britain and France. As far as the reparations and financial concessions which Germany was to make were concerned, Italy, for the very reason that it was the weakest of Germany's creditors, had a moderating attitude, which helps to explain why, at a certain point, Britain and France ignored what Italy had to say; particularly because, although opposed to the financial concessions, Italy was ogling at Germany for political purposes and thus arousing suspicion in Paris. These inviting glances at Germany were entirely Mussolini's idea, and it was they, as Grandi and his colleagues realized only too well, that were preventing agreement on disarmament with France, and making it side with Britain once again, as it had done in 1928, thus isolating Italy.

But Mussolini's diplomatic considerations went hand in hand with others that were at least as important, connected with the fortunes of fascism in Europe. The Depression was demonstrating fascism's profound vitality and its capacity to spread. As early as 1926 Mussolini had pointed out its universal and not merely Italian character. In October 1930 (a few weeks earlier, the National Socialist Party in Germany had won an amazing victory at the polls) Mussolini said the same thing again, but much more violently. He demanded – with a few reservations – the revision of the peace treaties, and was obviously contrasting the rising fascist movement with the reactionary, counter-revolutionary, conservative world that was in decline – in other words, the socialist, liberal, democratic and masonic world. Once again he was clearly alluding to France.

The failure of Grandi's experiment, like the failure of some possible domestic developments of fascism, was definitely due to the Depression, which we must therefore consider more carefully.

6

THE DEPRESSION

THE Depression reached Italy from America in 1930, after Mussolini and his Minister of Finance, Mosconi, had deluded themselves, as so many others had done, that it would not reach Europe and indeed that it might have beneficial repercussions on the European economy in general and the Italian economy in particular. On the contrary, Italy was one of the countries hardest hit, because of the weakness and imbalance of its economy and because the world crisis was superimposed on the still-active crisis provoked by the revaluation of the lira. The process that had taken place in 1927–9 was repeated on a bigger scale.

The largest industries were able to recover faster and better than the other sectors of production. For them, the Depression reached its climax in 1932: between 1929 and 1932, industrial production dropped by more than a quarter. It then rose, and in 1935 it had almost returned to the level of 1929. The Depression encouraged the process of concentration to go even further. Once the critical year, 1932, had passed, the speed and completeness with which a firm recovered depended on its size. The state of financial ruin in which some firms found themselves accentuated this, because prices were adjusted to those of the firms in trouble, whose costs were the highest.

Small firms were indeed hit much harder than large ones. In 1933–6, while large firms (those with a capital of over 10 million) were already clearly active again, small firms (those with a capital of less than a million) were in deficit.

For the very smallest firms, and for the country in general, the worst of the Depression came in 1934–5. In farming the Depression had effects more or less like those it had on the small firms.

Official figures on real wages show that industrial wages stayed the same, whereas agricultural wages dropped. But the condition of the wage-earning and less prosperous classes, particularly in agriculture, was worse than these figures seem to show. Emigration practically ceased, with consequent disadvantages: there was more unemployment, and the budget suffered because emigrants were not sending money home. Between 1929 and 1932, industrial unemployment went up to three and a half times its previous level. Many factories were on short time; women tended to be employed instead of men. These things diminished real wages and improved the unemployment figures only on paper. Food consumption declined, though not at a constant rate, and so quite definitely did the number of calories consumed per person. It has been calculated that the average standard of living went down by about 20 per cent between 1925 and 1932.

In order to alleviate suffering, the programme of public works was intensified, in Italy as elsewhere. The amount spent was smaller, in actual figures, than that spent in the same period in Britain, the United States and France; but if the relative poverty of Italy is borne in mind, it was similar in scope. Public expenditure, which went up sharply in 1931–2, involved a further increase in taxation. In 1931–4 this was more than 5 per cent higher than the already high level it had reached in 1922–5, with a clear increase in taxes on consumption. On the eve of the Second World War taxes had almost doubled since 1913–14. This increase in taxation was not enough, from 1931–2 onwards, to cover the increase in government spending, and to a growing extent the public debt was successfully used. Consolidated funds at 5 per cent were converted into redeemable stock at 3½ per cent. The state's budget again had a serious deficit.

But the policy of supporting the lira was not abandoned, although the fall in international prices, the devaluation of the pound in 1931 and of the dollar in 1933, and high public expenditure, made the effects of this policy weigh more heavily on the Italian economy. The tendency, already existing in 1927, for greater support to be given to large industries importing raw materials than to the exporting textile industry, became stronger. Very likely Mussolini's persistence in defending the lira was a result not merely of considerations of prestige but of the need to protect savers, who were buying government bonds. When, after 1931, the state began increasingly to use loans to cover public expenditure, this became all the more important. The hypothesis will have to be checked, of course, bearing in mind the fact that the most knowledgeable people in industry were beginning to look more and more askance at the high rate of the lira.

An economic policy of public intervention was demanded very forcefully by two sectors of production: the agricultural entrepreneurs who had suffered most from deflation at home and the protectionism that was increasingly being used outside Italy, and who were asking the state to regulate trade with other countries by a system of balanced exchanges and preferential customs-duties, a system which would help them in exporting and would protect them from the rivalry of foreign cattle-producers; and the iron and steel firms, the ship-builders and ship-owners, who used the widening crisis as an excuse to renew their traditional demands for public hand-outs.

Leading figures in Confindustria, on the other hand, until 1930 stressed the importance of containing taxes and expenses (this was done the same year by reducing wages and salaries). They viewed with traditional suspicion any possible intervention by the state in their affairs; they wanted trade with foreign countries to remain substantially free, restricted only by customs-duties, and no restriction on the import of raw materials, no international agreements to bind them to foreign firms much more powerful than themselves. In the preceding years this free-trading attitude had, in the economic field, corresponded to what had been revisionism in the political field : both were methods of avoiding the consolidation of the *status quo* and relationships with foreign power-groups, on both the economic and the political level. But in 1931, spurred on by the Depression, industrialists asked for state intervention to save those firms which were having the greatest difficulties.

State intervention in the country's economic life took three forms in 1931–4 : the setting up of IMI and IRI,* the establishment of consortiums, and the control of new industrial enterprises. The establishment of IRI in particular helped to save the firms in worst financial trouble, especially in the areas of engineering, shipyards, shipping companies, and investment banks – that is, the Banca Commerciale, the Credito Italiano and the Banco di Roma. With this policy the fascist government was in some ways following, rather than initiating, trends which were already to be seen abroad. But in Italy, because of the particularly concentrated character of the economy, life-saving operations, and therefore the enlargement of the public sector, were particularly noticeable.

IMI and IRI had a number of positive aspects. Fundamentally, they were not meant to spread public expenditure,

*IMI – Instituto Mobiliare Italiano – the channel for state loans to industry; IRI – Instituto per la Recostruzione Industriale – set up to provide money for banks and for industrial enterprises. [Translator's note.]

which in 1922–32 had already been intended for industrial life-saving, even further, but rather to give the state a means of controlling this expenditure, which ceased to be a simple fact and became the object of a conscious economic policy. IMI and IRI also had the beneficial effect of freeing some of the capital of industrial firms which had been kept in the large banks, and making it available to small and medium-sized businessmen, thus helping new firms to come on to the market. The setting up of IMI and IRI seemed not only to cut the monopolistic links between the banks and some sectors of large-scale industry but also to have a stimulating effect – unlike that of *quota* 90 – on production. But this tendency was held closely in check by all the big industrialists who, squeezed by the crisis, kept IRI under their control and strengthened their monopolistic position, on the one hand by setting up consortiums and on the other by the control of investment in new industrial plant.

Consortiums (and later control exercised over new enterprises) were first of all suggested by the iron and steel industry. Other industrialists were suspicious of them because of the watch which the state said it wanted to keep over the consortiums themselves. What happened later proved that the industrialists' fears were unfounded. In practice the consortiums were cartels which helped to encourage the mergers of financially healthy firms, to keep the large, financially unhealthy ones on their feet, to cut out rivalries and to keep production on a scale suited to the market which was to absorb it. The activity of the syndicates in favour of large-scale industry was helped by the measures taken as early as November 1929, but strengthened in January 1933, which controlled industrial establishments, and declared that the setting up of new ones in future must be authorized by the government. As the bodies responsible for giving these authorizations were strictly controlled by the big industrialists, all potential competition was thus eliminated. In spite of the price paid by the whole community and by economic development itself for the monopolistic stand taken, the industrialists managed to exploit this state of affairs very cleverly. We have seen that in 1935 production was almost back to its 1929 level. But we must not forget that, after 1934, this renewal was due above all to rearmament.

Corporativism was, in fact, the ideology aimed at giving a doctrinal and general justification to these tendencies. What might be called its prehistory was a long one, lasting until at least 1934. The reason for this lay not only in its lack of clear ideas but in the double hostility met by the corporations – first among the workers, and then, above all, among the leaders of industry. Working-class opposition faded out between about 1926 and 1929. The industrialists' opposition remained.

In the early days the fascists used the words 'trade union' and 'corporation' interchangeably. At first, it was because their ideas were confused; but this was not the only reason. The actual term 'trade union' had an ambiguous meaning, depending on whether it was used by the industrialists or by the trade unionists of the fascist left. The industrialists preferred to talk of trade unionism rather than corporativism because the corporations did not come within the framework of trade union arrangements. On the other side, the left-wing fascists, who often had a revolutionary syndicalist background, were more occupied with social matters and preferred talking of (integral) trade unionism; whereas the other, more conservative fascists preferred to talk of corporativism. As the latter gradually gained ascendancy over the former, as working-class resistance (particularly strong in Turin) was gradually weakened, as the state was made progressively 'more fascist', people talked more of corporativism and less of trade unionism.

The breaking up of the unified trade union confederation favoured this tendency. It marked the beginning of the plans which led to the corporative laws of 20 March 1930. From about that time, until 1932-4, fairly lively and interesting ideas continued to appear among theorists of both left and right.

People argued over whether the corporations should be based on the firm or the trade union, whether they should be divided into work categories or apportioned to a single productive cycle. Together with the more totalitarian tendencies there were others which considered the problem of the entrepreneur's autonomy, together with tendencies which stressed the need for production; while others again more decisively faced the problem of how to blend this necessity with the necessity of distribution. Ugo Spirito, a philosopher of the school of Gentile and politically a left-wing fascist, believed that the corporations ought to own the means of production, and that gradually the state itself would come to be identified with the corporations: a Utopian idea with some interesting points about it, such as, for instance, the need it affirmed for a planned political economy and for a kind of 'technological revolution'.

Spirito's ideas on left-wing corporativism appeared in 1927 and were extended in the years that followed, until 1934, in an effort to answer the Depression; but they were crushed by Mussolini and swept away by the Ethiopian war. The dominant tendency was for corporations to be linked to an entire productive cycle and, far from taking over Spirito's ideas, this emphasized the need for higher production. The first corporations to be established, in 1934, were of this type. This answered to a fundamental characteristic of fascism, which had always emphasized the fact that the problem of distribution must be subordinated to the problem of the production of wealth. The presence of the world Depression, far from encouraging Spirito's theories, increased this tendency.

In May 1931, in a speech to the Senate, Bottai said that he was worried about the low level of national income and the increase in capitalization, and that he believed the reasons for Italy's troubles were different from those in other countries. The world crisis, he went on to say, was a result of the unequal development of production in the world and the struggle between producers. From this he deduced that the Depression confirmed the fascist view which emphasized national rivalries instead of the class struggle. He went on to say that whereas in the United States and Canada, in Germany and Britain, the Depression was a result of over-production and excessive rationalization (and that therefore the way to overcome it was to cut out these excesses and then control the various factors of production with a slowing-down policy), in Italy there were quite contrary reasons for it and the way to overcome it and to reduce the deficit on the balance of trade was to increase and rationalize production. Addressing the industrialists, some of whose most notable representatives were in the Senate and who were anxious to suit production to the market in its critical condition, he praised the productivist policy (perhaps thus implying a criticism of quota 90) and emphasized the importance of acquiring new markets, with the help of the state.

Addressing the Chamber (where there were representatives of the working-class trade unions, as well as representatives of the leaders of industry), and, more to the point, addressing the workers, Bottai touched on another aspect of the matter. He regretted the fact that wages had dropped in 1930. The industrialists, he said, were wrong to neglect the demands of their workers, to regard the idea of corporations with suspicion and to see in them at most a means of achieving social peace – not a means of production. The workers, on the other hand, must further improve themselves in order to deserve a part in the increase of production, which corporativism in theory foresaw that they would have.

In July 1932 Bottai was dismissed as Minister of the Corporations and Mussolini took over the ministry himself. The economic policy of fascism had entered its interventionist phase. Mussolini wanted to show how important he considered the problem of corporativism, and, in this problem as in others, he tried to proceed with his usual sense of good timing. In October 1932 he even felt that capitalism (by which he meant a free-trade economy) might be in a position to overcome the world Depression. A year later he declared that capitalism was finished and that only corporativism was capable of overcoming it.

That year, the following events took place: Roosevelt was elected President of the USA, and an effort was made to find ideas similar to those of fascism in his economic and internal policies; nazism came to power and its analogies with fascism were obvious; fascist tendencies in general were spreading in Europe; above all, in internal affairs the interventionist economic policy was put into effect through the establishment of the IRI and substantially accepted by the industrialists. Mussolini, as a one-time socialist, had a stupid hatred of large economic concentrations and must have been glad to be able to declare in November 1934 that, after burying political liberalism, fascism was now burying economic liberalism.

Each corporation brought together the associations and unions of employers and workers belonging to a given productive cycle. The rigid subordination of workers to employers was strengthened in this way and, among employers, the weak were subordinated to the strong. Real power in the corporations lay with the representatives of Confindustria.

Another result was that the close links between these representatives and senior civil servants were strengthened.

The corporations' activity was the control of wages and salaries. In 1937 they were also given the task of supervising the carrying out of the provisions which said that new industrial plants must be set up under government licence. In January 1943 Bottai said (and his bitterness could be read between the lines) that, so far, the corporations were a long way from having achieved the task for which they had been brought into being.

The failure of corporativism was only one aspect of the failure of the entire fascist régime. The reasons for this failure were developing in the period 1929–32. The Depression, of course, had a decisive effect in stimulating it; but it would be hard to say (as has indeed been said) that the Depression was its only cause, without bearing in mind the fact that the fascist failure also had its roots in some of Mussolini's own ideas: the idea of solving domestic difficulties by a dynamic foreign policy, and the idea of making the institutions set up between 1926 and 1929 develop in a way that became progressively more totalitarian.

This latter problem also came to maturity in 1931. The masses had to be integrated into the state, not only as tools in the productive process (the treatment of the trade unions had already seen to that) but as citizens. They were thinking of young people, above all, who, it was said, must be given a myth which would bind them to fascism. This involved, in its intentions, the revival of certain aspects of left-wing fascism. In practice, a great deal of bureaucratic machinery was set up, greatly increasing the number of party members and developing the various organizations – youth groups, evening institutes, work clubs etc. The main function of this bureaucratic machinery was to serve as a stage to show off

Mussolini, and it confirmed something that was fundamental to fascism – its total lack of a sense of humour. A more important result was its political consequences : the fascist party, which had already been strictly subordinated to the state, ceased to function as a living organism and slipped quickly into an incurable hardening of the arteries and general decay.

This was the period in which Mussolini had Achille Starace as party secretary, for the ten years from December 1931. It was also a period which opened with that sign of the times – the School of Fascist Mysticism in Milan. Starace was said to be a good organizer. Intellectually, culturally and politically his complete lack of distinction was in contrast with the dubious but undeniable personalities of his immediate predecessors, Augusto Turati and Giovanni Giuriati.

Starace had the qualities of the courtier to a high degree. These were the qualities which Mussolini, perhaps unconsciously, was seeking more and more and which were appearing more and more – together with those of the profiteer – among high officials of the party and of the state. Mussolini did not want colleagues so much as men who would carry out his orders, and he was ready to turn a blind eye if many of them grew rich by more or less legal methods. The example of what was later called the Petacci gang and the secret traffic in gold organized, right in the middle of the war, by Marcello Petacci, with the connivance of officials high up in the fascist party, is typical.

Mussolini's sullen, authoritarian ways made him progressively more suspicious of any political personality, even a modest one. In 1932, Grandi and Bottai were, in practice, relieved of power. The same fate, indeed more noticeably, then struck the over-popular Balbo. Power was given to executors who could never overshadow Mussolini : to an efficient official like Arturo Bocchini, chief of police; later to an intriguer like Buffarini Guidi, Under-Secretary of the Interior. Count Galeazzo Ciano, who was later the most important of these powerful men and who also had a political personality, was in a sense the exception to this rule.

Relations between generals, businessmen, party officials, civil servants and courtiers bristled with calculating friendships, secret conflicts, resentments, jealousies, rancours, hatreds. Palace friendships, enmities and factions were formed and dissolved. Occasionally – not often, and quickly suppressed – violent scenes broke out suddenly. Often it all ended, at least for the time being, in hugs and smiles and offers of support and friendship. Mussolini knew perfectly well that these conflicts were going on. He put up with them, sometimes even encouraged them. He knew the art of setting man against man without seeming to, of keeping a solid group of men who depended on him and blackmailed one another. The conflicts among those around him helped to put him more and more above the fray.

There were conflicts, for instance, between Balbo and De Bono, between Lessona and De Bono again, between the senator Puricelli and the Scalera brothers, between Bottai, Balbo and Federzoni on the one hand, and Starace on the other, between Badoglio and Graziani, and between Badoglio again and De Bono. The conflicts connected with Badoglio were first apparent in 1929, those connected with Starace in 1932. The quarrel between Puricelli and the Scaleras was already serious in 1935, because of their rivalry over labour contracts for roads in East Africa. On the whole it can be said that the origin of these quarrels, which were very often linked to rivalry in seeking this or that favour from the state, date from 1930–31, with the declaration of the state's intervention in the economy, and that after 1935, with the expansion of this public intervention, they kept increasing. Typical is the case of Farinacci who, although he thundered against the economic groups in power, was always, it would appear, connected with the business underworld. After the introduction of state control over all foreign trade, in February –March 1935, Farinacci and a group of businessmen organized a group which, according to Confindustria, actually took a rake-off from firms (like Negroni, for instance) which applied for export licences.

It is not difficult to see fairly clearly, in this swarm of conflicts, two groups formed with the rise of Starace. On the one hand there were the moderates of fascism (except for De Bono) and the least irresponsible (like Balbo), supported by the most serious figures in the world of business and the army; on the other hand, the worst elements in the fascist leadership, and the most adventurous in the army and in business.

Mussolini himself in the end became a victim of the moral atmosphere created by fascism. His character was a mixture of cynicism and ingenuousness, and he ended up a prisoner of his own propaganda, actually believing what his flatterers told him, because he wanted to believe it. Gradually he, who had once so well divined the people's wishes, completely lost contact with the country. In the end he thought himself strong enough to impose upon it everything that it did not want: deprivation and, finally, a war which brought with it the most terrible devastation.

These tendencies came to dominate Mussolini's mind later, after the war in Ethiopia (the success of which intoxicated him), and especially after 1937. In the first half of the thirties these tendencies were being formed. An important stage was the ministerial changes in July 1932. Until then, although he was head of the government, Mussolini had behaved as *primus inter pares* towards the other ministers, whom he considered as active colleagues and with whom he discussed individual questions in a collegiate way, in the Council of Ministers. After July 1932 debate was used much less, and ministers became merely executors. Another stage came in 1934, when plans for disarmament had failed and the international situation had grown worse. During that year a close colleague of Mussolini's like Grandi ceased to address him with the familiar 'Dear Prime Minister' and instead used the fascist term 'Duce'. Farinacci's behaviour was different: he always aimed to be a kind of counter-attraction to Mussolini and in the years after the war in Ethiopia he continued to treat him with ostentatious familiarity.

From 1934 onwards, Mussolini stylized his own myth (one might almost say, his caricature) more and more, and in this Starace helped him a great deal: the carefully rehearsed expressions, tough, statue-like, the mask of an actor who ended by often wearing it even in private; his way, increasingly frequent in his public statements, of contracting his speeches into proclamations or even into mottoes.

All this happened under pressure from the Depression, which increased discontent at home and made fascist foreign policy more restless and aggressive. In those early years it had a function that was typical of Mussolini: to distract people from their troubles and to urge them to aim at greatness. This was achieved through the immense success of the Ethiopian war.

Under Mussolini, together with the high party officials and the senior civil servants who were closely linked with them, were to be found the majority of the upper middle class: old rich and new rich, eminent representatives of the world of business, the civil service, the army and the aristocracy. People were anxious to be given titles: this was something stimulated by a régime like the fascist one, which was largely based upon outward show and depended for its support a good deal on a strong band of parvenus.

Throughout the country, especially among the middle classes and in intellectual circles, the discontent brought about by the Depression showed itself in indifference, apathy and the swapping of funny stories. Lacking anything better – that is, the active support which it lacked – the régime fostered indifference and apathy.

In art, any reference to reality was strictly avoided unless it was affected and propagandist. For months Italian audiences were amused by a harmless little film comedy, *The Private Secretary*; and as an antidote to reality, they discovered the 'white telephone'.*

Writers were allowed to write, so long as they kept clear of reality and its problems. Formalistic writing was already beginning to dominate the post-war years, as a reaction against the culture of *Voce* (yet introduced by the final number of *Voce*). Sometimes this formalism, or rather this lack of commitment, had actually seemed to imply a protest against the gross reality of fascism. There was the eclectic review *Solaria*, in which two traditions were fairly clear: a literary one and a European one. Insofar as it implied a political protest, *Solaria* expressed a negative anti-fascism, which reflected very clearly the attitude of the best minds in Europe, summed up in Benda's *Trahison des clercs*.

In the twenties, the conscience of Italian intellectuals was reflected by a poet and a young novelist: Eugenio Montale and Alberto Moravia. Each in his own way and with his own methods had arrived at a similar representation of reality: repressed despair, resignation, ostentatious, bitter indifference, desolate landscapes full of cuttlefish bones and broken bottles.

Some scholars, above all historians, kept a sense of the civilized value of culture. In this field, the encouragement and guidance of Benedetto Croce was fundamental. In a nar-

* 'White telephone' films were the artificial, 'luxurious' films made at this time: a cinematic equivalent of the 'Anyone for tennis?' West End play. [Translator's note.]

rower field, the encouragement and guidance of Volpe were also extremely important in the progress of historical studies. Some scholars whose feelings were wholly anti-fascist called themselves followers of Croce, even though the most important one among them, Adolfo Omodeo, was originally a disciple of Gentile, as was Guido De Ruggero.

Other young historians, however – sometimes technically the most competent – preferred to waver, in culture and in politics, in a kind of cautious eclecticism that lay somewhere between Croce and Volpe. This eclecticism, which was explicitly approved of by Croce himself, was in the first place the result of a practical compromise; but it was also favoured to a remarkable degree by the common origins which, quite beyond the current conflict between fascism and anti-fascism and the revaluation which Croce was making of the upheavals made by the enlightenment in liberal civilization, brought together idealistic historicism, whether it was Croce's or Gentile's. The great *Enciclopedia Treccani*, edited with distinction by Gentile, symbolized very well the help which the main body of Croce's culture gave to Gentile's fascist culture.

A negative characteristic of historical culture at the time was that it wavered between the sometimes abstract moralizing of its anti-fascist representatives and the acquiescence, by the 'eclectics', in a historicism which passively accepted the *fait accompli*. These two opposite moral positions, both distorted though not equally serious, were both provoked by a single evil: the lack of freedom.

7

FROM THE DEPRESSION TO THE
WAR IN ETHIOPIA

THE Italian liberal state had been destroyed by the post-war crisis. With some exceptions, the other European states had managed to keep their free institutions. The world economic crisis now helped in a decisive fashion to bring great difficulties to the free institutions of many of these states, especially those in which liberal, democratic, political and social traditions were not deeply rooted and where there was least chance of economic recovery.

The difficulties and despair provoked by unemployment and poverty sent the masses either to communism or to movements on the extreme right. The base on which the liberal institutions stood became smaller and smaller. Finding themselves at the crossroads, the ruling classes almost everywhere ended by supporting the extreme right-wing movements. In Spain and France, however, in the early days, a large left-wing majority was formed, known as the Popular Front.

In some states, authoritarian systems were inspired mainly by Catholicism and Catholic corporativism; in others, particularly Germany, they were definitely anti-Christian, indeed tending towards paganism. Nearly always they declared themselves anti-semitic, to a greater or lesser degree. In Germany, nazism tried to rouse the national feeling of the people to anger; in other states, movements tried essentially – sometimes merely – to use force against the social system then in existence.

Only in Italy and Germany did fascism assume its most complete and typical forms, totalitarian in domestic policy and violently aggressive in foreign policy. At the roots of this were some structural aspects of Italian and German society and some special situations in foreign affairs. As far as the structural aspects were concerned, Italy and Germany were industrialized, mass societies which, because of their special (and dissimilar) historical limitations, had not been in a position fully to integrate the bourgeoisie, in town and country. When society found itself faced with a particularly serious crisis – the post-war years in Italy, the great economic depression in Germany – the bourgeoisie proposed, and the dominant groups accepted, a solution unlike classic conservatism : in other words, fascism.

As far as foreign policy was concerned, in Germany the victory of nazism was determined not only by the economic crisis but by anger, which had never disappeared, at the Treaty of Versailles. The same sort of thing had happened in Italy, where fascism made great play of the myth of the 'wasted victory'. Where these structural aspects did not exist (that is, in societies either more or less developed than the German and the Italian), and where there was no connection between these structural aspects and the problems of foreign policy, fascism did not prevail in its full sense. Yet there were fascist-style régimes which, in their various ways, were reactionary and authoritarian : Dollfuss's in Austria, Franco's in Spain, and those established in a number of countries in the Danube and Balkan area. In these latter countries, true fascism came to power during the Second World War as a result of the more or less direct domination of Nazi Germany.

Although fascism enjoyed a privileged situation in both Italy and Germany, its actual conditions differed a great deal in the two countries. In Germany, nazism was able to use totalitarian and imperialistic measures with a vigour and thoroughness unknown to Italian fascism. Fascism, as I said had been a reactionary régime that was typical of the twenties, whereas nazism hastened to become the reactionary régime typical of the thirties. Substantially, the Depression helped Italian fascism to decay and to become the launching pad for German nazism. It was the element which allowed Mussolini to make explicit the imperialistic substance of fascism without realizing clearly enough that fascist imperialism could advance only in proportion to the way in which the far more powerful Nazi imperialism was developing.

In 1932, however, thanks to the world economic crisis, the fortunes of fascism, after ten years of government in Italy, were clearly in the ascendant throughout the world. At home, too, the *Decennale* celebrations had strengthened the régime. On the other hand, the economic situation continued to grow worse and Grandi's foreign policy had been a failure. Mussolini then began to develop the outline of a plan that was to come into its own in the Ethiopian war and the years that followed it: a plan which gave priority to foreign policy, as a means, among other things, of settling difficulties at home. For this reason, in July 1932, he himself again took over the Foreign Ministry. A few months later, in October, he said: 'In ten years' time Europe will be fascist or being made fascist.' In the same year the entry on 'Fascism' in the *Enciclopedia Treccani*, written partly by Gentile and signed by Mussolini, appeared: there, the warlike, dynamic nature of fascism was exalted, although on a theoretical plane. The following year Mussolini also took over the three ministries of the armed forces.

In July 1932 he believed that war would break out in Europe around 1940, presumably (it would seem) between the western powers and the USSR. At that time he did not wish for war in the least, since it would hamper the achievement of his programme of public works. A few months later the Council of Ministers decided to reduce military spending, running at about 575 million, in the budget of 1933-4, and to increase what was spent on public works and education, to about 220 million. But the prospect of war made Grandi's foreign policy, which had played into the hands of Britain and France and taken from Italy any chance of an autonomous initiative, even more disastrous, according to Mussolini. The prospect of war, deplorable though it might be as such, was also a great opportunity for Italy to open up a broad field of diplomatic action.

Mussolini's attitude in 1934 went even further in the same direction, when he realized with sincere anxiety, indeed with dismay, that the plans for disarmament had definitely foundered and that the prospect of war was once again looming up in Europe. As I said, the big expenditure on public works ceased in 1934. On the other hand, Mussolini realized that the prospect of war favoured his usual policy of combining threats and agreement to a remarkable degree. A few days after hearing, worriedly, of the failure of disarmament, he was exalting the beauty of war in the Chamber. There was talk of 'moral rearmament' and of the fact that the fascist citizen and the soldier were as one. In September pre- and post-military training was introduced and, in schools, something known as 'military culture'.

In 1932 Mussolini had no intention of going back on Grandi's policy of agreement with the two western powers in the field of disarmament and of the League of Nations. The fact that Baron Aloisi, Mussolini's authoritative head of the Foreign Ministry, and the Under-Secretary Suvich were both well known for their pro-French views, makes this clear : Aloisi was also a delegate to the League of Nations. But Mussolini meant to carry on with Grandi's policy while at the same time giving more attention to Germany – a fundamental piece in the game, which gave Italy freedom of action and allowed it to put pressure upon France.

This was even clearer after Hitler came to power, when the

Italian and fascist connection became more valuable to the ruling classes in Britain and France, and it was seen – indeed people made an effort to see – that Mussolini's moderate fascism was an antidote not merely to the communist danger but also, and above all, to the kind of fascism exalted by Hitler.

Germany's presence allowed Mussolini to revive and to intensify the foreign policy he had used a little in 1928; a policy which could permit itself the luxury of being peaceable because it had the means to put pressure on the powers most anxious to keep the peace. It was also – at least it appeared to be – a rewarding policy, particularly considering the way in which France, in January 1935, half admitted that Italy could have a free hand in Ethiopia. In fact these rewards were spoiled by the decisive presence of Nazi Germany in the background. The years 1932–5 were the period in which Mussolini, Aloisi and Suvich light-heartedly and imprudently exploited an international situation that was particularly favourable to Italy.

It was an international situation now weighed down by the threat of war. In March 1933 Japan, which had attacked China in 1931, left the League of Nations, to be followed in October by Germany, which also left the Disarmament Conference. The following year the Austrian question came up. In July the chancellor, Dollfuss, was murdered by the Nazis.

In Italy there were signs of a deep-seated revisionism, but it was a kind that tried to differentiate itself quite clearly from the German brand, while at the same time exploiting it. In December 1933, soon after Germany had left the League of Nations, the fascist Grand Council said that it would be right for Italy to remain at the Assembly in Geneva only if it was radically reformed. In the same period, at a meeting of several hundred young Asians in Rome, Mussolini spoke out against nationalism in the colonial world, attacking the capitalist, liberal civilization, exploiter of Asia and at the time in a state of crisis, and comparing it with fascism's desire to collaborate with the East. These efforts to take advantage of national movements among colonial peoples, efforts that were anti-British and anti-French in intention, were in contrast to the repression some years earlier (which came to an end in 1931) of the Senussi movement in Cyrenaica. The repression had been so harsh that indignation had been expressed, and protests made, all over the Moslem world, and the Italian government had had to call on the two western governments for support.

In spite of all this, the foreign policy pursued by Mussolini between 1932 and 1935 was, as I said, a peaceable one. The fundamental diplomatic event of 1933 was the Four-Power Pact between Britain, Germany, Italy and France, drafted by Mussolini and Ramsay Macdonald in March and signed in the summer. Mussolini intended this pact to carry forward and make more effective some of the decisions taken in the Locarno Pact in 1925; a Locarno Pact interpreted as combining the principle of collaboration between the four powers with that of the division of Europe into spheres of influence. It was to be a means by which the four powers could run Europe in order to proceed by mutual consent, once the question of disarmament had been dealt with, to a revision of the current international situation: a revision that would be peaceful in Europe, and radical in Ethiopia. In concrete terms, what Mussolini wished to obtain from the others signatories of the Pact was a free hand in Ethiopia and even more, the recognition of Italy's leadership in the Danube and Balkan area. But Britain refused the concession he asked for on Ethiopia, and France, under pressure from the goverments which had signed the Little Entente, refused the concession on the Danube and Balkan area. Thus the Four-Power Pact, with its positive and its negative aspects, was never put into operation.

Mussolini tried to get the USSR to take part in the Pact, even indirectly. In September the non-aggression pact between Italy and the Soviet Union was signed. Mussolini's policy towards Russia (confirmed a year later when he supported the entry of the USSR into the League of Nations) had three objectives: to broaden what, for a fleeting moment, might appear to be the concept of Europe reborn; to manoeuvre the Russian pawn so that eventually it might be useful to his revisionistic aims; and, above all, to turn it against France.

In October 1933, as I said, Germany left the League of Nations and the Disarmament Conference. Mussolini, supported by Britain, tried to smooth things over, to allow Germany the right of parity in armaments and to help its return to membership of the League of Nations. France stood firm, and Mussolini was persuaded by Germany's mounting pressure on Austria that it was not wise to continue with his efforts. 1934 and the early months of 1935 were a period in which Italy came even closer to Britain and France.

Twice, in February and in September 1934, identical communiqués were put out by Britain, France and Italy, on the independence of Austria. In July there was a plan, which Mussolini supported, for an eastern Locarno pact. That same July came the putsch in Vienna. Mussolini would have liked to hold firm, although the king was against a war with Germany. Britain and France, whose love for peace equalled their fear of war, made it known that they would not follow Italy in the event of war. The Stresa conference in April 1935 was the high point of Mussolini's pro-western policy. Agreement was reached there on the position Britain, France and Italy were to take in favour of Austrian independence and against German rearmament.

But Mussolini's mind was now no longer occupied entirely with the Austrian question. In July of the previous year he had seen that if there had been a definite crisis on that question, Britain and France would not have become involved. This must have helped to make him shelve the question. Another matter that helped to move him away from his pro-western policy was the naval agreement which Britain alone sought and drew up with Germany (it was the start of 'appeasement') at the time of the Stresa conference. Besides this, two things had already happened in 1934 which, after France's refusal at the time of the Four-Power Pact, gradually made Mussolini put aside his plans for leadership in the Danube and Balkan area: first, the clearly anti-revisionist attitude of all the countries except for Austria, Hungary and Bulgaria; secondly, the definitive failure of the Disarmament Conference, that is, of the premiss that would allow for the much wished-for, peaceful revision of the *status quo* in Europe.

Having put aside his plans for the Danube and the Balkan area (or, more precisely, having limited them to the consolidation of his influence in Austria and Hungary, in order to control German pressure there), Mussolini turned his attention to Ethiopia. The conquest of it could not be put off any longer, now that, after the failure of the Disarmament Conference and the rearming of Germany, the threat of a new war in Europe had come very much closer. Mussolini's view on this differed from that of the king, the industrialists, the Chief of Staff Badoglio, the diplomatists and senior fascist officials, all of whom were worried about the difficulties of war with Ethiopia and afraid that it would weaken Italy's position in Europe, particularly considering the danger of the *Anschluss*.

Italy lacked Britain's tacit agreement, and it was a serious mistake for Mussolini and his colleagues not to have been sufficiently concerned about this, after the refusal on Ethiopia which they had been given at the time of the Four-Power

Pact. France, unlike Britain, had more than once made it clear that it would be in its own interest to turn the pressure of fascist Italy on to Ethiopia. In the past, Mussolini had rejected these semi-invitations, which he saw as a trap to weaken Italy's activity in the Danube and Balkan area. Now that he had abandoned the idea of this activity, he considered France's attitude once again. Agreement was reached, with Laval, in January 1935; an ambiguous agreement, because Laval did not say if his concession applied to armed intervention, and Mussolini interpreted his silence in the broadest possible way.

The decision to solve what was called the Ethiopian Problem was taken by Mussolini after consideration not only of foreign policy but of domestic affairs as well. The situation at home was worse than it had been at any time since 1927. People all over the country felt indifferent to the régime, detached from it. In order to overcome these feelings, in order to galvanize the masses and try to break the vicious circle of economic crisis, more drastic and more attractive measures were needed than public works (now, in any case, shelved), social and corporative propaganda, and the anti-capitalist pressure which the fascist trade unionists had been putting on at the end of 1934 and the beginning of 1935 (perhaps encouraged by Mussolini in view of the war, in order to emphasize its 'proletarian' character). In 1934, the policy of deflation, which the agricultural entrepreneurs could no longer sustain, had had to be abandoned. A tendency towards inflation, although only a small one, was beginning to appear and was endangering the whole basis of the economic policy followed since 1926; this threatened to alienate the people from the régime more than ever.

Economically the war came at just the right moment. The year before the war was, for most Italians, the one in which the Depression struck hardest, whereas the large firms were already clearly on the way to recovery. The Ethiopian war coincided with a period of general improvement; it became part of this improvement, and stimulated it.

The war was a great success from two points of view: the military and, even more, that of domestic policy. Mussolini presented the enterprise as a war that a poor country was waging in order to obtain a minimum degree of prosperity for its children. The kind of propaganda already used at the time of the war in Libya ('The great proletariat is on the move') worked perfectly for Mussolini. The war in Ethiopia gave him a platform for the kind of propaganda which fascism, born of nationalism, liked to use: a propaganda which transposed the idea of the struggle between the classes to one of a struggle between poor nations and rich nations. Every class in Italy felt it could see the truth of this, and proudly felt both proletarian and fascist. For a few months the identification of 'Italian' with 'fascist', which had been proclaimed for about the past ten years, seemed a true one.

All this was due partly to Mussolini's demagogic skill and talent for propaganda. But it was due even more to the attitude of Britain and the League of Nations. Their opposition to Mussolini's intervention in Ethiopia gave the Italian people a sense of suffering and injustice and was the decisive element in making them rally round the fascist government. The result was that no colonial war had ever been so popular in Italy. The people accepted the motives for the war put forward by the régime; it also altered them – in a way that was sometimes contrary to official directives – to its own image and likeness. Italian kindliness on this occasion prevailed over fascist ferocity.

Fascism put the war forward as one of conquest and the people as one whose spirit was that of the conqueror. Admittedly there were many incidents of great cruelty during the war, the violence of which stood out all the more clearly owing to the fact that the enemy was almost defenceless. But the Italians felt no racial pride in being white. For months, in both Africa and Italy, a popular song was *Faccetta Nera* (Little Black Face). The official, propagandist view of the slavery from which barbarous Ethiopia was to be freed was extended: the Italian was going to Africa not simply to free the little dark girl, *Faccetta Nera*, from slavery, but also to link her to his own destiny and – why not? – to court her in an Italian sort of way. No difference was noticed between a poor Abyssinian girl and a poor Italian boy. It seems that Mussolini disapproved of the song and in the early days thought of banning it.

Even the diplomatic conduct of the war, which was typical of Mussolini, had tremendous success. In spite of opposition, led by Britain, in the League of Nations, Mussolini got everything he wanted: Ethiopia and the Empire. He played his cards well and pulled every possible string in international relations, without ever allowing it to snap. Although it did not appear to do so, in 1935 the British government did its best to abandon Ethiopia. It was forced to take a firm line, however, by outraged public opinion at home. But the most important of the economic sanctions, the one on petrol, was not applied, nor was the Suez Canal closed to Italian ships. The failure of these two moves, particularly the petrol sanction, allowed Mussolini to carry on to victory.

The British government wished to avoid war with Italy at all costs, not only, and not so much, because the conservatives, who were then in power, had a liking for fascism, but because of the weakness of the British navy after years of disarmament. This weakness made such a war seem completely out of the question to the government in London. Although the British would certainly have won, they would have had to fight without military support from France, and would have been further weakened in the face of two other threats, considered far more serious: Japan and Germany. Through his secret services Mussolini knew how weak the British navy had become, and he exploited this knowledge to the full. The policy of disarmament, which he had supported with such conviction in previous years, now allowed him to finish his Ethiopian enterprise with complete success.

In spite of Mussolini's formally tough tone in speaking of the matter, the Ethiopian conflict might have been settled through a diplomatic compromise, if an arrangement put forward by the British and French governments had gone ahead. Substantially this aimed at ensuring Italy the economic exploitation of Ethiopia, while leaving the Emperor as formal sovereign there. It was a matter of giving Italy a kind of mandate over Ethiopia.

What prevented this from going ahead, and increased Mussolini's toughness and gathered the Italian people round him, was the anti-fascism of the British, who, outraged at his premeditated attack on a defenceless people, forced their government to withdraw the plan. Thus the war took on, and confirmed, its typical characteristics: on the one hand it was an anachronistic colonial enterprise and the no less anachronistic formal founding of an empire; on the other, it was the first great conflict on an international level between fascism and anti-fascism, opposing sides which would appear very much more clearly quite soon in the Spanish Civil War.

During the twenties, when fascism was on the crest of the wave, the anti-fascist exiles had wearily repeated the old themes of protest or had made individual gestures of protest. The communists were a group on their own. This situation appeared to change as soon as the Depression began to have an effect on fascism and to favour its capacity to spread. In some of the most advanced anti-fascist circles outside Italy people began more and more to become aware of the irrevocably European character of fascism. In January 1932 the revolutionary and, as Carlo Rosselli called it, post-fascist programme was formulated – the movement Giustizia e Libertà (Justice and Freedom). The need was stressed to bring anti-fascism out of its substantially negative attitude, to make it mature into a concrete alternative to fascism, in other words to lay the basis of the Resistance.

During the years that followed, this need was amply confirmed by the way in which the international situation developed. 1933 was the year in which Hitler came to power, 1934 the year in which plans for disarmament decisively failed. Nazi Germany was on the way to becoming a great military power – and very quickly. The horror of war, the premonitory signs of which had already appeared in the Far East, was now looming over Europe. To defend itself against nazi Germany and to gain western support became the prime motives of Soviet diplomacy; the latter motive, however, always being disappointed. The results of this, whether direct or indirect, were very important in anti-fascist circles. In France, the foundations of the Popular Front were being laid, justified domestically as a defence against the ever-increasing pressures of the extreme right. The Italian socialist and communist parties put their old quarrels aside and made an agreement to act together. Giustizia e Libertà claimed to be a fully autonomous movement, quite outside the disbanded *Concentrazione antifascista*.

With Mazzini-like vigour, Carlo Rosselli spoke of 'post-fascism'. Palmiro Togliatti gave a concrete idea of what a part of post-fascism might be and sketched the outlines of a communist party that would make use of the experience which fascism imposed on Italy in organizing large masses of people. However, anti-fascism never lost, indeed it accentuated, the composite character which was seriously to limit its capacity to govern Italy after the end of the Second World War.

The development of anti-fascism took place within a wider cultural context. Those years of opposition on an international level between fascism and anti-fascism, war and peace, were also a crucially important period in the cultural field. It might be said that the ideological tendencies, mostly conservative at bottom, which had dominated European culture since the end of the nineteenth century and which, more or less distorted, had been the cultural matrices of fascism, disappeared; and that new tendencies, politically more committed and basically anti-fascist, took over from them. The anti-fascist intellectuals – Benedetto Croce in the first place – to some extent anticipated this change; Gramsci, in prison, was developing the themes of a robust, original marxism. The war in Spain, in which cultural forces were mostly lined up in defence of democracy against the rebellion of General Franco, was the first great practical manifestation of these new ideological tendencies.

In Italy many intellectuals, who during the twenties had reflected the attitude of Benda, in the thirties showed a progressively more conscious degree of anti-fascism. In the field of art a need was felt for closer contact with the reality of Italian life (something that was to be developed further in the years after the Liberation). The discovery of the American novel showed this in literature, and Visconti's film *Ossessione* (*Obsession*) showed it in the cinema. While Montale's *Ossi di seppia* (*Cuttlefish Bones*) and Moravia's *Gli indifferenti* (*The Time of Indifference*) had expressed the conscience of Italian intellectuals during the period when fascism was in the ascendant, at the end of its twenty years this conscience was expressed through works like Visconti's film and Elio Vittorini's *Conversazione in Sicilia*: manifestations of a conscious 'political' protest against fascism and war.

8

FROM THE WAR IN ETHIOPIA TO
THE SECOND WORLD WAR:
THE SITUATION AT HOME

THE economic policy of the régime between the war in Ethiopia and the Second World War continued to operate in favour of the Italian upper middle classes. Economic interventionist policies, which earlier in fascist days had aroused perplexity in industrialists, were, as we have seen, accepted, with good grace or bad, after the war in Ethiopia. This was the period – beginning in February 1935 – in which interventionism in trade with foreign nations became much greater and later, after sanctions, produced what was known as autarky.

A strict control of international trade and payments was justified by similar tendencies which had appeared abroad, and by the deficiency in gold reserves, which had begun with the deflationary policy and had then become more and more severe, in spite of the devaluation of the lira in October 1936. It is interesting to note that autarky did not fail to produce friction with Italy's German ally, who watched it with displeasure because it wished to see the Italian economy as purely agricultural, and complementary, that is subordinate, to the German economy.

Autarky was intended to limit consumption and to channel resources into industrial investments. A war economy was essential, one that became part of the war effort which had been started by Italian industry in 1935 and helped to get Italy out of its economic difficulties. From 1937 onwards the level of production was higher than it had been in 1929.

But, while bearing in mind the ability of Italian industrialists, we must not forget that the recovery was determined largely by the war effort. In this effort, the Italian economy came third, after the German and the Japanese. Nor must we forget the high prices, the waste, the imbalances, the consolidation of positions of monopoly which were nearly always parasitic, provoked by autarky. Between 1920 and 1929 Italian industry had increased production by 60 per cent, which was higher than the average achieved in the countries of western Europe; whereas between 1929 and 1939 the increase was only 15 per cent, 'lower, for the first time since 1900, than the average for the agricultural and industrial countries of western Europe' (Romeo).

Not all industrialists gave autarky an equally warm welcome. It seems that those most hostile to it were the less concentrated industries, those most interested in exporting, such as the textile industry, the importance of which continued to decrease compared with industry as a whole. Until 1935 the textile industry had taken on more workers than any other, but after 1935 it was the engineering industries that did so. The more concentrated industries, those most linked to public expenditure, were particularly in favour of autarky.

The firms best able to profit from the autarkic régime, and the easy terms given to favour self-financing, were those which had been most dynamic in previous years : particularly electrical firms, chemical firms (Montecatini, Snia Viscosa, Agip) and Fiat. In order to develop the iron and steel industry IRI set up a large financing body, Finsider, in 1937. Experts are far from agreed on the merits of this. According to some, between 1937 and 1943 Finsider was a parasitic body, radically different from the one which later, during the fifties, greatly developed the iron and steel industry. According to others, in the years 1937–43, although it could not function properly because of the difficulties created by the war, Finsider was the vital seed of future developments. However, in the plans made for home production not only the chemical but the iron and steel industries had to take on a leading role. It is significant that in 1938, contrary to what had happened in the past, the interests of the electrical firms were sacrificed to those of the iron and steel and chemical firms, which at last managed to get electrical tariffs contained.

Until the Ethiopian war the economic forces showed little wish to support the expansionist aspirations of fascism; whereas now things changed, because the economic basis of imperialism became the armaments industries, those favourites of autarky. Until the Ethiopian war the economic basis of imperialism had substantially remained what it had been before 1914 – the export of capital, which Italian economic power groups were only moderately keen on. Besides, the representatives of financial capital had preferred to guard their interests abroad not so much by a policy of strength as by keeping up friendly political relations with countries, like Yugoslavia for instance, with which they had close economic ties.

Autarky gave a strong stimulus to industrial concentration. The large firms were favoured by the control of trade, and so were the consortiums. Import licences were granted only to the largest industries, which also enjoyed special terms for exporting. In 1939 there were more than 10,000 public companies in Italy. More than three-quarters of their capital was concentrated in 500 of them, or 5 per cent of the total, and these 500 often had links with one another. Here are some figures which are no less awesome in the light of the small degree of inflation then operating : Edison, the giant electricity firm, increased its capital from 1350 million in

1934 to 2000 million in 1941; Montecatini moved from 500 million to 1300 million in 1938; Snia Viscosa, from 525 million in 1937 to 1050 million in 1941; and the capital of Finsider amounted to 1800 million in 1940.

The IRI grew in importance. It had been established in 1933 mainly to prop up firms in danger, but in 1936–7 it took on a new function, that of administration. This, it would seem, was due to the efforts of its chairman, Beneduce, a skilful financier who had learned his business under Nitti; its object was to prevent IRI being used primarily by industrial adventurers like Puricelli who wished to shift their losses on to the public and keep their profits for private gain.

It seems likely that Beneduce intended the IRI to become the tool of an economic policy which, together with its traditionally productivist aspects, would have others which would be part of a plan to produce a development less unbalanced than that of the previous years. A number of symptoms seem to confirm that this was not an isolated idea: some fascists (such as the party deputy-secretary, Dino Gardini) regarded Keynes with interest; and, even more significantly, the Minister of Finance, Revel, sought to maintain the balance between global incomes and the availability of goods, and to rationalize the tax system and provide it with methods of predicting and checking which would almost automatically allow it to adapt levels of taxation to the variations in revenue.

A month after Beneduce's proposal, in March 1936, Mussolini publicly announced the programme for autarky and for an economic policy which anticipated the existence of a 'master plan'. Whether he meant, at state level, to absorb some of the ideas of left-wing fascism (such as those of Spirito), or whether he was following Beneduce's suggestion, is a matter that needs further study.

The IRI did indeed do something to curb imbalances, such as strengthening the iron and steel and mechanical engineering industries in Naples. But its function was not so much that as to develop state control in certain key industries affecting defence, autarky and the empire. Its function was not so much to nationalize the strategic industries and sectors of industry, as to nationalize the industries whose ability to expand was exhausted, or which were not in a position to make profits. It is significant that the electrical industry remained in private hands; and it is equally significant that the IRI gave back, into private hands, the properties which it had acquired, thus giving up a means of lightening the burden which the income they produced placed upon the country's development. Nevertheless, even with these limitations, the reform of the IRI in 1936–7 was a matter of central importance in the development and modernization of the Italian economy.

In spite of Beneduce and Revel's efforts, autarky made for imbalance. In relation to industry, property was put at a disadvantage in particular by some fiscal measures taken against it in 1936. Once again, cracks began to show in the alliance between industrialists and landowners. The conflict, smoothed out in 1922 and settled in 1925, had reappeared during the first half of the thirties and had once again been settled when the industrialists had accepted industrial controls. Admittedly, during the whole of the fascist period taxes weighed more heavily on property than on industry. But, to make up for this, beween 1926 and 1934 the policy of supporting the lira had favoured unearned incomes rather than profits. After the war in Ethiopia property which produced unearned income no longer had this compensating privilege.

Businessmen and tradesmen also felt that they had been

sacrificed for the sake of the industrialists. Autarky increased their problems, which for several years, ever since the consortiums were set up, had been pressing. They saw in sales consortiums a tool of the large industries and hoped that these consortiums would be subordinated to the corporations, which in theory should have been the mediators between the various branches of production.

The greatest imbalance, however, was in wages. Admittedly, when the war in Ethiopia began, workers' insurance was reformed and improved. But the main means by which the war itself, and autarky, were paid for was through inflation, although this was modest and always kept under control by the Minister of Finance. The rise in prices meant a transfer of wealth from incomes based on labour to profits. The strikes in March 1943, although provoked by the disasters of the war, could be traced back to this transfer of wealth. The workers' wages fell throughout the period 1934 to 1939. In 1939, they were back almost at their 1913 level. The way in which income was distributed among the wage-earning classes and the other classes was, until 1934, similar to that which existed in 1913. Between 1934 and 1939, this pattern of distribution changed, to the disadvantage of the wage-earning classes. Although it appears that income per head went up between 1936 and 1939, the increase was concentrated in the higher income groups, whereas in the lower it remained below the level of 1929.

If we are to have an idea of the way in which wage-earners, and the poorest classes in general, lived, other elements must be considered as well. Taxes continued to rise, and, between 1934 and 1937, rose particularly fast, particularly indirect taxation. The daily consumption of calories per person continued to go down until about 1937. Between 1934 and 1938 Italy was one of the worst countries in Europe (in eighteenth place) as far as the daily intake of calories per person was concerned. The period of the Ethiopian war and the end of the Depression was a particularly hard one for the mass of the people, owing to the low pay and the high level of indirect taxation. But the reality was perhaps less black than statistics of wages may suggest, because unemployment was fairly low. From 1937 onwards, the situation improved: consumption clearly increased and indirect taxation became slightly lower than direct taxation (although taxes as a whole were increased). A policy of demographic colonization was introduced in Libya and 3550 families were settled there; for a while, land drainage works were taken up again. In 1939, wages were increased.

In spite of this uneven progress, the basic tendency was for a greater difference in income between those in the large industries and everyone else. The rise in prices hindered Mussolini's policy of concentrating financial resources in the public sector – thus giving the state the greatest degree of autonomy – and helped to make the state a mere intermediary through which these resources were passed on to industry. Certain aspects similar to those which had characterized economic conduct in the First World War began to appear. The objective of channelling resources to the large firms had always been a fundamental aspect of fascism's economic policy. In the past the government had been forced to curb the polarization of incomes, first with public works, then with the war in Ethiopia. Autarky had been meant to take up and indeed to develop the balancing function which public works had been given in the past few years, promoting full employment in a country poor in raw materials, like Italy. Some successes in employment were indeed achieved, but these were outweighed by the drop in wages.

Towards the end of the fascist period Italian society showed deep divisions in its structure, which highlighted the disintegrating character of the fascist party and of the state which it had created.

General instability and uneasiness were all the greater since not only the working classes but even the upper middle classes were moving away from the régime, in spite of the favourable treatment given to the big industrialists. The enthusiasm aroused by the war in Ethiopia was soon over. In 1937 the division between fascism and the country began to reappear and grew decisively wider in the following year. The new factor was that this division now penetrated ever larger areas of the conservative world: the upper middle classes, the Vatican, the court.

Economic policy, as I said, continued to operate in favour of the big industrialists, who deserted the régime only at the end of 1942, when it had in fact already been swept away. The attitude of conservatives towards foreign policy was different, however. As the issue was more and more clearly becoming that of peace or war, the importance of foreign policy was decisive. Apart from the prospect of a general war, the war in Spain and the haemorrhage of military and financial expenditure which it involved were decisive factors; so was the use that could be made of the Empire which, because of the effort it involved, was worsening the crisis in Italian finance.

In 1937 Mussolini's faults as a man became more glaring, and from then onwards took on a ferocity that was actually pathological. In March, his trip to Libya became a noisy manifestation of Anglophobia in the name of the rights of Islam, of which Mussolini claimed to be the protector.

Even formally, the process of 'making the state fascist' was given its final touches. The Ministry of Press and Propaganda became the Minister of Popular Culture, for instance, and the National Fascist Institute of Culture (presided over by Gentile until then) became the National Institute of Fascist Culture. The blow dealt to liberal institutions by the speech on 3 January 1925 was emphasized and exalted far more than it had been so far: on 3 January 1938 the anniversary became a national holiday. Almost at the same time the use of the pronoun 'voi'* became obligatory and the 'passo romano'† was introduced into the armed forces.

The orders on 'voi' and on the 'passo romano' were part of Mussolini's wish to 'temper' the Italians' character, as he put it. Later, during the war, he even reached the point of occasionally welcoming the terrible air-raids by the British and Americans on Italian towns, because – he said – they would help to strengthen the Italians' character. We do not know how far this was an aberration, pure and simple, in Mussolini, or how far it may have come from a mask of optimism with which he tried to face up to reality. Fascism moved towards its end in a special atmosphere, which was, as has so often been said, a mixture of farce and tragedy.

In the course of 1938 (which was the year in which Europe decisively turned to war) two events – one connected with foreign policy, the other with home affairs – helped to alienate a section of the conservatives from the régime: the Anschluss, or union of Germany and Austria, and the declaration of a campaign against the Jews.

The motives which made Mussolini take on racialism were various: the wish to imitate his powerful ally Germany; the hope of giving Italians a 'racial' awareness (he had not, perhaps, forgotten Faccetta Nera); and, above all, the wish to give the country's discontent an outlet in Jew-baiting.

It has been said that fascist anti-semitism was improvised and gratuitous, and not justified by the reality in Italy. In fact, a doctrine like racialism ought to have been repugnant to the doctrinal origins of fascism, which were idealistic

*'voi' replaced 'lei' as the formal pronoun, being considered by Mussolini to be more noble. [Translator's note.]

† The Italian version of the 'goosestep'. [Translator's note.]

Above all, it has been said, anti-semitism in Italy was not justified by the pre-eminence of Jews in the world of finance and business, which they had in other countries.

All this is true. But it must be remembered that fascism had always emphasized the subordinate nature of theory as opposed to the creativeness – that is, the improvisation – of action. It should also be borne in mind that although there was no explicitly, violently anti-semitic tradition in Italy, there was, in respectable, petty bourgeois circles, a hidden anti-semitism of Catholic origin. Jews were mentioned with a sly smile. Margherita Sarfatti, who was Jewish, had been Mussolini's mistress. But from his very first years in power Mussolini had always shown his colleagues this winking, leering form of anti-semitism. Thunder against the so-called Jewish plutocracy, too, had always been a favourite weapon of official fascism.

With the 'voi' and the 'passo romano' Mussolini thought he could temper the Italians' character; with racialism, he tried using one of his traditional methods – that is, arousing the mob instincts. But the mob no longer responded. Even among fascists the anti-semitic campaign was ill received; particularly was this so in the case of the elderly Gentile and the more moderate fascist leaders like Emilio De Bono, Federzoni and Balbo. Balbo had moved from the extreme fascism of his youth to an attitude that was anti-German and critical of the régime (probably for reasons of personal discontent). But racialism, as officially proclaimed by the fascists, helped to alienate, above all, the Church and the Vatican.

Relations with the monarchy were deteriorating, too. The conflict between Mussolini and fascism on the one hand, and the king and the monarchy on the other, which had come into being some time earlier, during 1937, became obvious in March and April 1938. Mussolini created (without, it would appear, consulting the king) a title of Marshal of the Empire, which he conferred upon the king and upon himself. The king was upset at being placed on the same level as Mussolini, and this gaffe meant the end of the friendly collaboration which had existed between them, substantially without interruption, since October 1922. It did not mean, however, that the king broke with fascism. With the majority of the industrialists, indeed even more noticeably, he hung back prudently when changes were made and up to the very last moment tried to curb any tendency to make him break with the fascist régime.

Mussolini reacted angrily to any tendency towards a change. Things were now growing dangerous, for the increasingly wide division between the conservatives and the régime corresponded to the increasing difficulty which the régime was finding in acting as mediator between the classes. Mussolini's reaction was to bring out, once again, the violently anti-bourgeois slogans of the early days of fascism. It is not surprising that this was in marked contrast with a greatly increased effort at industrial concentration. The social slogans ('Forward with the people' in 1931, 'Cut down differences' in 1934) which Mussolini had used in times of acute economic trouble, or even, as in 1934, when social differences were tending to widen, had a similar character.

What was new about his attitude was the fact that, whereas in 1931 and 1934 the slogans started from the unspoken presupposition that there was a close link between the régime and the bourgeoisie, and that these slogans were seeking to strengthen the bourgeois position of leadership of the masses, Mussolini now declared that the link between the régime and the bourgeoisie had been broken, and no longer bothered to assure them that they were leaders of the working class. This return to some of the extremist, subversive themes of fascism, with its connected rhetoric of war and empire, was very likely due to Mussolini's awareness that war was coming; and, in its turn, it may have had some importance in later making him enter the war on the side of Germany.

9

FROM THE WAR IN ETHIOPIA TO
THE SECOND WORLD WAR:
FOREIGN POLICY

AN article by Giuseppe Bottai, written in 1935, during the war in Ethiopia, clearly set down the aspirations of fascist foreign policy as expressed in the African campaign. Beyond this war, Bottai said, lay the European conflicts brought into being by the peace treaties. The present war was a prelude to the breaking up of the Treaty of Versailles, to the destruction and subversion of the present international order.

After wavering for a long time, between moderate revisionism and radical revisionism, Mussolini's diplomacy settled decisively for the latter. It would be far fetched and inaccurate, however, to deduce with hindsight that from 1936 onwards he irrevocably took the road to war. Admittedly the mirage of a great victorious war and of military victory smiled at him more and more. Certainly his instinct told him, more and more, that Europe was going to become involved in a war. But it was not imminent. For the present he confined himself to carrying on with the policy he had used with such dazzling success at the time of the Ethiopian war; that is, straining Italy's relations with Britain and France as much as possible, being quite sure that they would not be broken.

During the war in Ethiopia and the diplomatic tussle with the League of Nations and with Britain, relations with Germany, although improving, had not got beyond a state of evasive caution. Germany had shown sympathy for Ethiopia and had sent it arms.

In the past Mussolini had seen Germany as the fundamental piece in some future revisionist chess game, but with Germany he had combined two other states which were unhappy over the peace treaties – the USSR and Turkey. And eventual revisionist policy based on these two states would have had the great advantage of not favouring – even indirectly – Germany's own revisionist ideas on its southern borders, that is, towards Austria and the Brenner. But neither Turkey nor the USSR had ever shown that it meant to prop up fascist revisionism, even in its most moderate version. Turkey had drawn away from Italy in the early thirties, when fascist revisionism seemed to be centred on the Balkans. The USSR had drawn away from Italy after the Ethiopian war, and the Spanish Civil War had strengthened this decision.

Fascist diplomacy was now centred decisively upon Berlin. A really radical revisionism implied close collaboration with Germany. The big question which divided the two powers was that of Austria. Mussolini hastened to get rid of it by giving way to German pressure. In June 1936, a few weeks after the end of the war in Africa, he asked the Austrian government to deal directly with Germany. It was a clear sign that he was no longer prepared to defend Austrian independence. This was a serious decision, for it meant that Italy actually gave up the most important result of its victory in the First World War. The German, Nazi empire was going to weigh heavily upon the Brenner and upon Trieste.

Mussolini's decision has also been seen and criticized as a typical diplomatic volte-face. This is not true. Right from 1925 he had examined the possibility of eventually giving way on the question of the *Anschluss*, in the eventuality of a general revision of the state of Europe; a revision which was, indeed, now taking place. More typical of his diplomacy was the fact that he kept open all possible solutions to the Austrian question, veering violently from one to another:

from direct opposition to the Anschluss to acceptance of it.

This is the place in which to deal briefly with the young Foreign Minister, Mussolini's son-in-law Galeazzo Ciano, who was considered to be a kind of heir to the régime.

Galeazzo Ciano's father, Commandante Costanzo Ciano, had held important posts in Mussolini's government and was one of the most typical figures of the régime. It was said that in a short time he had amassed a large fortune, thanks to his political power. Certainly the Cianos knew the value of wealth and social prestige. While Mussolini never forgot his working-class origins and considered his contact with the traditional ruling classes as a more collaboration, Galeazzo Ciano (whose father, born into the middle class, had had himself made a count) felt profoundly connected with the ruling classes. Of the two faces of fascism – the subversive and the conservative – he accepted only the conservative, being a typical second-generation product, one of those men whose fathers had come up from nothing or nearly nothing and had amassed power and riches.

The worst aspects of Ciano's character were his conformity and his cynicism. His relations with his wife, Edda Mussolini, were often stormy, but Ciano, who did not hide his Catholic feelings, had for his father and for all his family the sincere affection which the conformist has for the founder of his dynasty. At the same time, he accepted state crime without batting an eyelid: he it was, apparently, who ordered the murder of Carlo Rosselli; and King Zog of Albania was to have been murdered on his orders. But there was more to Count Ciano than that: he faced death, when it came, firmly and with dignity. Ambitious, intelligent and worldly, stubborn and self-centred, he lacked the capacity to see deeply into things and to free himself, in his work, from a rather brilliant amateurishness. As Foreign Minister he could not rise to the height of the dramatic situations which he himself created.

Ciano ended up by disapproving more and more of Mussolini's attitudes, in both foreign policy and home affairs. But – and this is quite understandable – it took him a long time to free himself from the fascination which his all-powerful father-in-law exercised over him and to take on a secretly critical attitude towards him and towards his anti-bourgeois, bellicose and pro-German tirades.

In the last four months of 1937 Ciano, as his *Diary* shows, was filled with euphoria, with bellicose, anti-bourgeois and anti-British feelings, and was all for the Duce and for Germany. He became suspicious of Germany after the *Anschluss* in March 1938, and again after the annexation of Bohemia to Germany in March 1939, then finally and decisively so in August 1939, after the Salzburg meeting, when the German decision to start the war was unexpectedly revealed to him by von Ribbentrop and Hitler. Even on the two earlier occasions Ciano had been wounded, above all, by the discourteous behaviour of his German ally; the Germans had taken dramatic decisions on their own initiative and had told him about them only after the event. But the surprise at Salzburg should not be attributed entirely to Hitler and von Ribbentrop's behaviour with regard to Italy. It was the fault of Italian diplomacy not to have realized the possible consequences of the treaties between Germany and the Soviet Union, treaties which Italian diplomatists certainly knew about.

After these events Ciano tried to act as a brake upon Mussolini's aggressive, pro-German behaviour. Yet both before and after them Ciano not only carried out his father-in-law's orders (as was natural) but interpreted them in a particularly dynamic way.

In July 1936, after only a few days at the Foreign Ministry, Ciano urged Mussolini to intervene in the Spanish Civil

War. The King was opposed to intervention. The war in Ethiopia had been over only two months; the country badly needed a rest, and so, in particular, did its finances; from the diplomatic point of view it was very dangerous to put European attitudes to the test a second time in so short a time. But, encouraged by Ciano, and passing through what seemed like a manic phase of euphoric activity, Mussolini thought the war in Spain would soon be over, leaving fascist Italy higher than ever in prestige, and dominating the western Mediterranean. He was also attracted by the character which the Spanish conflict quickly took on: it was an ideological war between European fascism and anti-fascism.

Italian intervention in Spain was, in the long run, an obvious failure. Only on one point – and that a fairly important one – was Mussolini proved right: he saw that the western democracies, afraid of finding a red republic in Spain, only half-helped the legitimate government and in this way, part willing and part unwilling, contributed to the victory of General Franco and of fascism. But it was a long, exhausting war, in which Italian resources in military equipment and money were worn thin. The diplomatic advantages Mussolini had hoped for never came, or came on a very small scale, because Franco cunningly proved to be a less pliable ally than he had been believed to be in Rome.

At the time of their intervention in Spain, Mussolini and Ciano strengthened their relations with Berlin, which became close and cordial; so much so that in October 1936 they were given the name of the Rome–Berlin Axis. 1937, from the diplomatic point of view, saw these relations become even closer, and in November this resulted in the Tripartite Pact between Germany, Italy and Japan. The Pact was officially aimed against the USSR (Anti-Comintern Pact), but Ciano interpreted it as being aimed, in reality, against Britain.

Ciano's attitude had some significance not only on the

level of international relations but at home as well. Traditional Italian friendliness towards England was beginning to appear again among the upper middle classes, and the king let Mussolini know of this tendency. Even earlier, in June 1937, the king had put gentle pressure on him to modify his enthusiasm for Germany.

Mussolini himself was not unaware of these attitudes. The close relations between Rome and Berlin had been compared with an axis in order to emphasize their non-exclusive character, to show that they were open to collaboration with other states. It was Ciano who, from the time of the *Anschluss*, insisted on the need to integrate relations between Italy and Germany into a general scheme of collaboration with other states, which would counterbalance Germany. These states were sometimes Britain and France, sometimes Spain and the countries in the Danube and Balkan area.

Thoughts of this latter area, it will be remembered, had been shelved in 1934 by Mussolini, who was wholly taken up with the question of Ethiopia and later with that of Spain. It is likely that one of the reasons for the new approach to Yugoslavia, which concluded with a treaty of friendship in 1937, was the wish to get the country out of the ever tighter, though at present only economic, grip of Germany. Ciano's policy towards Yugoslavia continued to reflect exactly the ambivalence which Mussolini had always shown towards it. The friendship of 1937 was followed during the war by the destruction of the Yugoslavian state, something which was first considered as early as August 1939, was the plan to annex Croatia.

It was, in fact, in this area that Ciano meant to find a counterweight to Germany, not only with the diplomatic collaboration of the countries there but also by taking some of them – such as Albania, Yugoslavia and Greece – over and occupying them militarily. This exemplifies my earlier remark that sometimes, even after 1938, he interpreted his father-in-law's directives in a particularly dynamic way. Ciano was steeped in fascism; he deluded himself that he could make himself a counterweight to the brutal power of Germany while rejecting the use of Nazi methods.

The dismay caused by the *Anschluss*, and immediately afterwards, in April 1938, the secret anger aroused by Germany's attitude to the question of the Alto Adige, hastened the approaches being made to Britain, and in the same month, on 16 April, an agreement between Britain and Italy was signed in Rome. At the same time, similar approaches were made to France. But Hitler's visit to Italy early in May reinforced Mussolini's pro-German attitude and ruined the agreement which Ciano was beginning to come to with the western democracies. On this occasion, in order not to spoil his relations with Britain and the approaches being made to France, Ciano managed to decline the German offer of a formal treaty of alliance (which was to become the Pact of Steel in May 1939).

A few months later, in the summer of 1938, Hitler's annexation of the Sudeten territories seemed to fling Europe into disaster. Mussolini, like Hitler, now wanted war. But, whereas Hitler wanted it as soon as possible and was even ready to start it at once, Mussolini preferred to postpone it for five or six years. Although he did not realize the whole tragic gravity of the problem, he knew that Italy was unprepared to face a war, both militarily and financially.

For this reason he approved of his son-in-law's attitude. Ciano was seeking not to ruin relations with London and Paris irreparably. So, when the crisis of the Sudeten territories broke, he did all he could to settle the matter peaceably and arranged a meeting in Munich. Mussolini was pleased with his success. The western world and the Italians breathed a sigh of relief. On his return to Rome from Munich, Mussolini was greeted by the enthusiasm of crowds which perhaps appeared to him the largest in the whole fascist period. He was not really pleased, however, and met them with a gesture of slight annoyance. The Italians were clearly determined not to become a warlike people.

The decision, taken in June 1938, to hold the World Fair in Rome in 1942 was an answer to a number of the objectives which Mussolini had in mind. It would show Italy's peaceful intentions, both to the western democracies, to reassure them, and to Germany, to hold it back. It would increase the prestige of fascism. And it would improve the financial situation by bringing foreign currency into the Fair. Having achieved this last object, Mussolini felt he would be ready for war.

In the meantime, as far as the western democracies were concerned, he continued to use his familiar tactics; in fact he exaggerated them. He kept asking for more and more, either because he was sure that the democracies, in order to keep on the right side of Italy and avoid disaster, would give way in the end, or else because war had now been decided upon and sooner or later it was going to break out. This behaviour was directed in particular at France. With Britain, Mussolini was rather more anxious to maintain good relations; but even this seemed a lost hope when Neville Chamberlain and Lord Halifax visited Rome early in 1939 and their visit came to nothing.

Once again, then, the idea of making a formal alliance with Germany was considered. Ciano saw the occupation of Bohemia as a second, and unwelcome, surprise. But the need somehow to balance the ever-increasing power of Germany in some way made him take advantage of the upheaval in the diplomatic world, caused by the German action, to occupy Albania, militarily, in April 1939. The following month the Pact of Steel was signed with Germany.

Mussolini, who calculated that he would be ready for war in 1943-4, immediately told Hitler (while later curbing efforts for peace which the Queen of Italy was making)* that it would be impossible for Italy to take part in a war for the next three years. Three months later, in August, Ciano learnt in Salzburg of the German decision to attack Poland within the next few days. This meant war.

It has been said that after the occupation of Bohemia, Italian diplomacy was divided into two strands, a pro-German minority, and a majority, which included Ciano, Giuseppe Bastianini, Under-Secretary at the Foreign Office, and Bernardo Attolico, ambassador in Berlin, favouring an agreement with Britain. Ciano's actions, however, do not entirely correspond to this presumed tendency, at least until the Salzburg meeting. But after that meeting, he became clearly anti-German and opposed the war, taking the side of Balbo, Bottai and Grandi on this fundamental question.

Mussolini's reaction was different. After the Salzburg meeting his first impulse had been to take part in the war at Germany's side. He was torn between the longing to do this and the material impossibility of doing it, because of Italy's lack of preparation for war.

Only the navy was in a good state. The army and the air force's condition was deplorable, and yet funds for military expenditure had been settled at 133 thousand million lire. This disastrous situation was due essentially to poor organization, dishonesty (how much of that 133 thousand million had really been spent on the objects for which it was intended?) and above all by the lack of raw materials. This lack of raw materials was in its turn due to the disastrous currency situation.

*According to Nino D'Aroma, contacts were made in November–December 1939, in particular with the Belgian Royal Family, in order to bring about an international peace conference.

It was a bitter pill for Mussolini to swallow; yet he had to declare that Italy, which at least in theory was so belligerent and so fascist, was not going to fight. The feeling of inferiority felt by so many Italians towards Germany was in him becoming enormous. Originally he had not really liked Germany; he had been educated, rather, to favour France. But in spite of his occasional anti-German outbursts, he had become desperately attached to it; partly because of the personal esteem which Hitler had shown for him (always cleverly knowing how to deal with him and where to find his weak points), and partly because of resentment against France. Contempt from the Germans, nourished by the memory of Italy's turn-about in 1914–15, frightened him. It is said that, during the meeting at which it was decided not to fight, he said several times in German : 'Betrayal ! Betrayal !'

Having declared Italy's non-belligerence, Mussolini was still uncertain within himself. Then he planned to bring Italy into the war in the spring of 1940. He was obsessed by the thought of defending the prestige of fascist Italy, and by the fear of being thought to have betrayed his ally. After a visit to Rome by von Ribbentrop in the spring of 1940, he took the decision to enter the war on 10–11 March. The quick, sensational fall of France was the deciding factor for Mussolini.

Everyone, or nearly everyone, in those days saw Germany as the winner. Everyone, or nearly everyone (not Ciano, however), now thought the war would be very short. The king, too, favoured entry into it. The conservatives were supporting the régime again. Italy had to qualify for a stake in what was happening, in order to avoid losing the advantages to fascism of the victory in France, and in order to prevent Germany being victorious on its own and weighing heavily upon Italy, perhaps even occupying it militarily.

It was now that Mussolini's errors of diplomatic judgement came home to roost.

EPILOGUE

ONLY during the first months of the war was Italy allowed a little initiative of its own in its diplomatic activity. From the end of 1940 it was at the mercy of the Allies and of Germany. Ciano used those early chances of action above all to try to balance German superiority.

In August 1940 Italy would have liked to direct its action, not against Britain, but against Yugoslavia and Greece. But Germany refused to allow this and said that it was necessary to concentrate all efforts against Britain. Still in August, and then later in December and January, there were efforts by the Italians and the Soviet Union to counterbalance German influence in the Balkans. These efforts, too, were halted by Germany. The Italian attack on Greece, which began on 28 October, was decided upon, against Germany's wishes, as an implicit reply to Hitler's occupation of Rumania. The campaign in Greece was an appalling military failure, saved only, to the mortification of Italy, when Germany came in to occupy Yugoslavia militarily and imposed peace upon Greece.

The campaign in Greece in the winter of 1940–41 was important not only from the military and diplomatic point of view but because it helped, perhaps decisively, to widen the gap between the country in general and the régime that governed it. Some of the more shrewd and moderate fascists, such as Grandi, in February–March 1941 began to look for some way of getting the country, and themselves, away from the Duce's régime.

Mussolini's reaction to the gap which appeared more and more clearly between fascism and the country was a violent one. But what is striking about this reaction is the total lack in it, not merely of any moral grandeur, but even of intelligence; Mussolini's incapacity to examine his conscience and to make any kind of political analysis of what was happening. His reactions were as violent as they were crude, superficial and impotent.

All that really happened was that his contempt for people turned into resentment; he felt resentment towards the king and the upper middle classes, on whom he had showered so many favours and who now, as he saw it, were repaying him so ungratefully; he felt resentment towards his generals, party officials and senior civil servants, who he now realized had deceived him when, to keep him happy, they had praised Italy's non-existent preparedness for war (in this, the main victim of the cringing attitudes imposed by Mussolini was Mussolini himself): he felt resentment towards the Vatican and the priests, against whom the old anti-clerical spirit in him occasionally longed to launch an offensive, the traditional feelings of his native region, the Romagna, encouraging him to do so; finally, at times he felt resentment towards the Germans, either because of some particular treacherous act of theirs, or because of the peril which, quite objectively, their enormous power meant for Italy.

From all this anti-bourgeois, anti-monarchical and anti-clerical resentment the Italian people as a whole were excluded, not so much because Mussolini failed to notice their hostility to the régime (it appeared quite clearly to him during 1942), as because their attitude was, at least on the surface, more passive and because it was not considered politically important (the strikes in March 1943 came as a bitter surprise). There is no doubt that the resentment he felt aroused Mussolini's old socialist, or socialist-inclined, spirit, and helped to prepare what was later to be the attitude of the Salò Republic in social matters. In the period 1943–5 the tendencies which had been appearing since 1937 came to full maturity : the two components of fascism – the moderately conservative and the extreme – split and were in opposition to each other; the moderately conservative part gathered round the monarchy and later round the Vatican and the Catholic party; the extremist side produced the Salò Republic, which remained an empty dream, like the fascism of 1919.

During the war relations with the Germans, although warm on the surface, were not in fact friendly. There was no liking between the two peoples, only fear and constraint on the one hand, contempt on the other. Even between the leaders and high party officials of the two countries there was friction. Germany did not always keep its promises to provide industrial supplies or coal, whereas it was more than prompt in importing food supplies from the Italian countryside.

Sometimes Mussolini played the part of the Germans' official defender, sometimes he burst out violently against them. Gradually, as time went by, the power and prestige of Germany and Hitler became more and more crushing, compared with the power and prestige of Italy and Mussolini. Mussolini was caught between resentment – mixed with secret envy – of his ally and the need to rush in to support him whatever he did, for fear of being later cut out from the spoils of victory.

During the war Mussolini tended to live more than ever from day to day. It would seem that thoughts of the future brought problems that terrified him. His state of mind veered continually and chaotically between states of high and low spirits, between illusion and disappointment, depending on the military situation. Ciano, too, although much more moderately, went through these same ups and downs. Illusion reached its height in June 1942, at the time of Rommel's offensive in Libya.

1942 was also the decisive year of the war. In October–November (from their defeat at El Alamein to the American landing) the Italian and German positions collapsed on the North African front. The British and Americans began massive bombing raids on the towns of northern Italy. In December, the Italians were overwhelmed on the Russian front. In the same period the conditions that were to lead to the fall of fascism, brought about by the king and some of the leading fascist party officials, were secretly being prepared.

At that time – January 1943 – a significant conflict took place between Mussolini and Ciano. Ciano was now convinced of the need to get out of the German alliance and to make peace with some of the enemy powers. Mussolini, too, twice realized that there was a chance of making peace with some of the Allies. But as far as he was concerned any eventual moves must be made with the full agreement of Germany. Besides, whereas Ciano wanted to come to some compromise with the western democracies and together concentrate their efforts against Soviet Russia, Mussolini wanted to come to a compromise with the USSR and carry on the war against the western democracies. Mussolini proposed this to Hitler, who refused it, twice: the first time in December 1942, at the time of the Italian collapse on the Russian front; the second time in March 1943.

The war was making conditions of life more and more intolerable, especially in northern Italy. The average calorie consumption per head had fallen to about 2,000, about a fifth less than it had been before the war. In the towns, the decrease was much greater. To hunger were added even more terrible sufferings of all kinds, physical and psychological, caused by the air-raids. The sharpened discontent of the ordinary people against the war and the régime was, among workers in the industrial north, developing a political meaning and awareness. In March 1943, for the first time in eighteen years, there were strikes in the factories of Turin, in the working-class circles which had been among the last to give way to fascism between 1926 and 1928. Explicitly these strikes occurred for economic reasons but implicitly they were political. They should be seen as the prelude to the partisan Resistance.

The differences between Mussolini and Ciano on matters of diplomacy became part of the manoeuvres taking place to rid the government of Mussolini.

Three plots were being organized at the same time: there was the plot of moderate fascists, led by Grandi, who wished for a formally constitutional self-transformation of fascism into a parliamentary régime; there was the army plot, led by Badoglio, hoping for a military *coup d'état*; and there was the plot of moderate anti-fascists, led by Bonomi. The king chose Badoglio's solution and used the plot devised by Grandi (a vote in the fascist Grand Council on 25–26 July 1943) to justify getting rid of Mussolini. It was a solution which, dominated as it was by fear of the Germans and by the wish to exclude all participation by the people in general, certainly boded ill for the future developments of Italian democracy. However, Badoglio's solution, merely because it implied a constitutional break (even if the king did not recognize it as such), turned out to be less damaging to the objectives of the future developments of Italian democracy than Grandi's would have been.

In September 1942 Ciano had a visit from Bottai. Bottai was known to belong to the fascist malcontents and did not hide his extreme uneasiness from Ciano; then, as if casually, he threw out the opinion that the war was illegal because it had been declared without previous consultation with the fascist Grand Council. Obviously Bottai (with Grandi's agreement) meant to sound Ciano out and see if he would come over to their side. But Ciano cut him short and said that the supposed illegality of the war being fought was a pointless quibble.

The military disasters of those months brought the plan to rid the government of Mussolini to fruition. The king, advised by the Minister of the Royal Household, Duke Acquarone, secretly made up his mind in January 1943. Mussolini heard something of what was going on and spoke to Ciano about it, making no effort to hide the suspicions he felt towards him. Ciano, who truly loved his father-in-law and who, it seems, was not yet wholly involved in the planned *coup*, appeared hurt by these suspicions.

He became involved on 15 January. In the days that followed the palace plot became clear. On 20 January Ciano gave Mussolini the chance to get away from Germany and to make contact with the western powers. Mussolini listened to him without a word. This cold silence was in itself an eloquent reply. The following day he told Ciano that he would not abandon Germany and that he had faith in its secret weapon (which was much talked about).

Father-in-law and son-in-law were now moving in two different directions. Ciano himself was becoming convinced of the need to get rid of Mussolini and saw the only chance of salvation in the monarchy and the Vatican. The king, who knew of his attitude, had always treated him, particularly in recent times, with affectionate, almost ostentatious, goodwill. The Vatican, whose prestige was rising the more the fascist state disintegrated, was the best channel through which eventually to get in touch with the United States.

On 5 February Ciano was dismissed from his post as Foreign Minister. He then at once expressed a wish to be made ambassador to the Holy See. Mussolini, who could not have liked the odd reasons for this choice, tried to dissuade him from it, but Ciano stood firm. Duke Acquarone hastened to congratulate him warmly.

In the same period Grandi was dismissed from the government (he was Minister of Justice) although he remained President of the Chamber of the Fasces and Corporations. The king gave him a decoration. These were not coincidences.

The net was closing round Mussolini, manoeuvred by Acquarone and Grandi. Perhaps his second plan for a separate peace with the Soviet Union, which he put forward in March, was partly intended to defeat these plots which, obscurely, he could sense.

But it was just an obscure feeling, nothing more, and he never really became aware of them. His surprise on 25 July remained just that – surprise – and he never managed to dominate it, to use it as a way of examining his conscience, or to turn his sterile resentment against 'traitors' into judgement and action.

The only pathetic note, particularly obvious in the final period, was Mussolini's loneliness in the Social Republic, his lack of a friend among all the courtiers, a lack which he himself seemed suddenly to realize in the days that followed the disaster of 25 July. Besides, Mussolini himself, being the tough actor he was, did not fail to exploit this pathos.

This is not the place to describe the bloodthirsty events of the Italian Social Republic. German domination forced the great majority of Italians, out of idealism and out of necessity, to resist. The Social Republic, between the German hammer and the partisan anvil, was merely a hanger-on, a supporter, of the Germans. In spite of the bloodthirstiness that dominated it, the Social Republic did make efforts (similar to those of the French Vichy government, but more timid) to lighten the weight of German pressure, both on the people interned in Germany and on the industrial wealth of northern Italy. These efforts met with little or no success.

Nor was the general activity with which Mussolini tried

to recapture public support any more successful. A tame opposition was allowed, and this seemed like a distant echo of Mussolini's statements before Matteotti's murder. The chaotic social programme of the fascist Republic recalled what was being done, in circles profoundly different, by other collaborating governments. In Petain's, the dominant note was one of paternalism, in Ante Pavelic's and Mussolini's it was demagogic.

Anyone who remembers the picture of Mussolini in that final period, with his weary, aged expression, his hollow cheeks and the sad, intense, almost astonished look in his eyes, cannot fail to feel pity. Yet he was unable to stop himself parodying the dramatic events through which he was living. To the end he was an actor, incapable of truth.

The rising in Milan found Mussolini hard-pressed, from close at hand. He said good-bye to one of his followers and made a kind of spiritual testament of it. As far as he himself was concerned, he said, his sacrifice was necessary and he was ready to accept it. His words seemed – and probably were – full of emotion. Perhaps at that very moment he was thinking of the plan to defend himself to the bitter end in Valtellina. We do not know whether, when he left Milan, he was hurrying to play his last card in the defence of Valtellina or fleeing to Switzerland. The partisans found him close to the Swiss border, disguised as a German.

BIBLIOGRAPHY

OF WORKS ON ITALIAN FASCISM IN
ENGLISH OR ENGLISH TRANSLATION

F. Carsten, *The Rise of Fascism*, Batsford, 1967, Methuen (University Paperbacks), 1970.

Ciano, *Ciano's Diary 1937–38*, Methuen, 1952.
Diary 1939–43.

F. W. Deakin, *The Brutal Friendship*, Weidenfeld & Nicolson, 1962; Penguin Books, 1966.

C. F. Delzell, *Mussolini's Enemies*, Princeton University Press, 1961.

Laura Ferma, *Mussolini*, Chicago University Press, 1961.

Sir Ivone Kirkpatrick, *Mussolini*, Odhams, 1964.

E. Nolte, *Three Faces of Fascism*, Holt, Rinehart & Winston, 1966; Mentor 1970.

A. Rossi, *The Rise of Italian Fascism*, Methuen, 1938.

G. Salvemini, *Prelude to the Second World War*, Gollancz, 1953.

C. Seton-Watson, *Italy from Liberalism to Fascism*, Methuen, 1967.

E. Wiskemann, *The Rome-Berlin Axis*, Collins, 1966.

E. Wiskemann, *Fascism in Italy*, Collins (Fontana), 1969.

S. J. Woolf, ed., *European Fascism*, Weidenfeld & Nicolson, 1968.

S. J. Woolf, ed., *The Nature of Fascism*, Weidenfeld & Nicolson, 1960.

MORE ABOUT PENGUINS
AND PELICANS

Penguinews, which appears every month, contains details of all the new books issued by Penguins as they are published. From time to time it is supplemented by *Penguins in Print*, which is a complete list of all titles available. (There are some five thousand of these.)

A specimen copy of *Penguinews* will be sent to you free on request. For a year's issues (including the complete lists) please send 50p if you live in the British Isles, or 75p if you live elsewhere. Just write to Dept EP, Penguin Books Ltd, Harmondsworth, Middlesex, enclosing a cheque or postal order, and your name will be added to the mailing list.

In the U.S.A.: For a complete list of books available from Penguin in the United States write to Dept CS, Penguin Books Inc., 7110 Ambassador Road, Baltimore, Maryland 21207.

In Canada: For a complete list of books available from Penguin in Canada write to Penguin Books Canada Ltd, 41 Steelcase Road West, Markham, Ontario.

St. Norbert College Library
DePere, WI